estherpress

Books for Courageous Women

ESTHER PRESS VISION

Publishing diverse voices that encourage and equip women to walk courageously in the light of God's truth for such a time as this.

BIBLICAL STATEMENT OF PURPOSE

"For if you keep silent at this time, relief and deliverance will rise for the Jews from another place, but you and your father's house will perish. And who knows whether you have not come to the kingdom for such a time as this?"

Esther 4:14 (ESV)

What people are saying about ...

Peace in the Waiting

"I don't believe I've ever read a book about the pain of loving people who don't know Jesus. My first question was, 'Why hasn't anyone written this already? It's so important!' June Chapman has given us a thorough, biblical exhortation to help us carry the pain of carrying our lost loved ones to Jesus. In doing so, she shows us that this is both our highest calling and our deepest place of trust. A stunning debut."

W. Lee Warren, MD, Christian
Book Award–winning author of
Hope Is the First Dose and host
of *The Dr. Lee Warren* podcast

"In *Peace in the Waiting*, I found comfort from someone who is where I am: in the middle of waiting for a loved one to come to know Christ. June not only normalizes the heartache we face but challenges us to *grow* rather than get stuck in the grief, to see that the waiting is not just about them; it's about us too."

Lynn Cowell, coauthor of *Esther: Seeing
Our Invisible God in an Uncertain World*

"June captures the heart of God in her writing. Her love for lost friends and family is eclipsed only by her passion for what Jesus can do in the lives of the unsaved. June wisely shows us our part in the story of redemption but reminds us that we are not the Redeemer."

Greg Wigfield, MDiv, former
chaplain to the Washington Redskins,
businessman, and retired pastor

"Peace in the Waiting is a vulnerable and heartfelt testimony of one believer's journey through grief, doubt, and frustration while longing for the salvation of loved ones. Chapman invites readers into her raw emotions and hard questions as she wrestles through deep pain to find hope in Christ alone. While salvation is God's domain, Chapman offers practical wisdom for how to wait—waiting with open hands, meditating on God's promises, and worshipping despite sorrow. This book will encourage all who ache for prodigals, providing empathy and spurring reliance on the faithful Father who pursues the lost."

Joe Carter, senior writer at the Gospel Coalition
and author of the *NIV Lifehacks Bible*

"June shares a struggle that most—I would argue *all*—followers of Christ are experiencing in these days: praying and waiting for loved ones to follow Jesus. This book is important for the church, and I know you will find yourself in her stories. Don't stop praying with urgency, know it's the Holy Spirit (not us) who transforms hearts, and allow Him to do what only He can do as you wait well."

Rebecca George, author of *Do the Thing:
Gospel-Centered Goals, Gumption, and Grace for the
Go-Getter Girl* and host of the *Radical Radiance* podcast

"June guides us through an honest journey of entrusting our closest family and friends to God. You'll walk away from reading *Peace in the Waiting* not only trusting the Lord more but better equipped to pray and love those in your life who don't yet know Him."

Nicole Jacobsmeyer, speaker and author
of *Take Back Your Joy: Fighting for Purpose
When Life Is More Than You Can Handle*

"With the compassion and care we need when tackling such a tender topic, June comes alongside us as an empathic friend who understands the struggle and knows how to offer the encouragement, wisdom, and *peace* we need to wait well. Full of practical steps and soul-strengthening prayer starters from beginning to end, *Peace in the Waiting* gently guides us down the rocky path of loving the lost by helping us address head-on the hard questions and thoughts that trip us up and unravel our peace. "

Meredith Houston Carr, JD, speaker,
writer for Proverbs 31 Ministries
Encouragement for Today devotions

PEACE
IN THE
Waiting

WHEN YOU
LOVE PEOPLE
WHO DON'T
LOVE GOD

JUNE CHAPMAN

ep

estherpress

Books for Courageous Women
from David C Cook

PEACE IN THE WAITING
Published by Esther Press,
an imprint of David C Cook
4050 Lee Vance Drive
Colorado Springs, CO 80918 U.S.A.

Integrity Music Limited, a Division of David C Cook
Brighton, East Sussex BN1 2RE, England

Details in some stories have been changed to protect
the identities of the persons involved.

Library of Congress Control Number 2023947654
ISBN 978-0-8307-8614-5
eISBN 978-0-8307-8629-9

The Team: Susan McPherson, Stephanie Bennett, Judy Gillispie,
Karissa Silvers, James Hershberger, Susan Murdock
Cover Design: Kim Burke

Printed in the United States of America
First Edition 2024

1 2 3 4 5 6 7 8 9 10

010524

*For my dear friends and family who
are yet separated from God—
children of the Most High King—
may you one day know the depth of
Christ's great love for you.*

Every prison has a door
Every captive can be free
Every sinner has a hope
And hope is rising up in me

"Hope Is Rising" by Luminate

Contents

Introduction

Every day for the past forty-nine months, I've prayed for my friend Charlotte. A self-described agnostic, she's convinced of neither the existence of an omnipotent God nor the infallibility of science to disprove the concept altogether. To Charlotte, there just isn't enough evidence one way or the other.

I've known her for about five years. We met at work and seldom saw each other—until a few months in, that is. Through project committees and mostly by happenstance, our paths ended up crossing regularly.

Charlotte loves music. She's a musician herself, and she follows a few artists loyally. That first year we worked together, one of her favorite artists came to perform in our city. It was a rare opportunity to attend a live performance. And it just so happened to be her birthday weekend. Charlotte bought tickets well in advance, planning to enjoy the night out with her friends. But it was around the holidays, and when the performance finally neared, it happened to fall on a day when her invited friends were traveling.

We didn't know each other too well at the time, and I mostly listen to music rather than watch it. But when she asked me if I would join her, I couldn't say no. I love live events, crowds, lights, noise, and excitement. I know those are odd things to enjoy, but I'm a raging extrovert.

She suggested burgers for dinner beforehand. Burgers and good company—I couldn't have planned a more ideal evening. It's funny how food, time, and proximity garner more friends than mutual interest or passion. I'd never even heard of this artist. I just had to show up. I enjoyed the performance so much I even bought the T-shirt.

Over the four years that followed, Charlotte and I became close friends. We kept showing up in each other's lives more and more, sneaking off together for breakfast sandwiches and coffee, leaving cartoon drawings on all the conference-room whiteboards, and fiercely battling in the office olympics.

As I got to know Charlotte, I appreciated ever more her intellectual brilliance, wit, and thoughtfulness toward others. Charlotte is, for lack of a better word, gentle. The kind of person who gives everyone the benefit of the doubt.

Even amid pandemic isolation in our city, we showed up for each other with patience and support. As a verbal processor, I talked circles around her, but Charlotte always listened and cared. We shared our fears, our small victories, and most importantly, our love of cats. She loved me well as a friend. And I hope I did the same for her.

I got to know Charlotte about as well as anyone could. We talked about things that hadn't come up at work. I learned about her sister and her extended family. I saw photos of all her childhood pets. I heard about her dream to one day move out of the city and own horses—a passion she explored when she was younger but hadn't been able to continue after her parents' divorce. We listened to a lot of music as well. Her favorites became my favorites.

There were some dark and confusing days too—times when we couldn't make sense of what was going on in the world. But we were patient and gracious with each other. We became as close as sisters.

If you've ever spent consistent one-on-one time with someone over a long period of time, be it a friend, neighbor, coworker, or family member, you understand how you come to know someone's greatest strengths and deepest weaknesses. You learn about the person's hopes and goals and dreams. You also experience the parts that are less than perfect. You see the vastness of human depravity—the parts that remind us why we need a Savior.

The good news is that we have one.

We have a Savior named Jesus who became God in the flesh, lived a perfect life that we could not live, and died on the cross, bearing our sin and shame on His shoulders. His sacrifice reconciled us to a perfect, holy God.

You and I know this intimately, so it's only natural that we long for our loved ones to know Jesus too. We are waiting for lives to be saved—to see the people we love repent of their sins and choose to follow Jesus as best they can all the days of their lives, with joyful hearts and obedient spirits. We desire that they would abide in Him, love His Word, and worship Him as Lord.

If you're reading this book, I imagine you are praying for a few loved ones today. Maybe you've been praying for a long time.

Perhaps you're like me, and you're praying for a close friend. Or perhaps you're a parent whose child has chosen a prodigal journey, despite your best efforts. Or maybe it's your parents, who are aging rapidly, and you're afraid of what comes next for them. Maybe you're thinking of your spouse who isn't walking in faith. So many kinds of relationships come to mind—neighbors, coworkers, coaches, mentors. Maybe you're even thinking of someone you don't particularly like. I know many believers who are praying for difficult people too.

I understand that this waiting comes with very real weariness. If you're feeling worn down during this season of prayerful waiting, you're not alone. Maybe you're exhausted, even struggling to find joy, like I was. You want to trust in God's perfect timing, to hope that change is possible, and to find assurance that you're doing enough. You deeply desire peace in this season of waiting, especially if it's going to last even longer.

The idea of life—let alone eternity—without these loved ones is unimaginable. I understand. I live in an increasingly post-religious city. Between my coworkers, neighbors, friends, and the other folks I see regularly, I have dozens of people in my life who don't anchor themselves with faith in Christ.

These people are His masterpieces. But we have something they do not: We have an active, abiding relationship with Jesus. A trust in a holy God. An awareness of sin that leads us to repentance. An assurance of eternal salvation.

When we know something so surely, so factually, so personally, it's challenging to understand why our friends, family members, spouses, children, neighbors, coworkers—our *people*—can't share this part of our world. Why do we get to know the way, the truth, and the life, but our people do not? And most importantly, when we share it with them, what do we do when they reject this message? What do we do when the people we love refuse to believe?

After years of sweet friendship and precious community with Charlotte, I had a few questions for God. I cried out to Him, wrestling with the convergence of facts I know to be true. I know that God fearfully and wonderfully made Charlotte. I know that God is good. I know He heard my prayers. And I know that He could soften Charlotte's heart and open her eyes not only to His existence but also to the depth of His great love. Yet from my perspective, it didn't look like anything had changed. Despite months of repeated pleading, and despite everything I *know* to be true, Charlotte still did not see the ultimate Truth.

After wrestling with God for several years, I've finally come to a place of peace. I'd like to help you do the same. In this book, we'll walk together through *the thoughts you might think and the questions you might ask* as you prayerfully wait for your loved ones to follow Jesus.

Our minds can invent a million barriers to peace in the waiting. I wish there were a simple way to attain it without exploring all the things that get in the way. Just when we've arrived at peace in one area, our minds offer another thought or question to consider. That's why we'll explore this season of waiting from many different angles.

This is a journey on which there are no easy solutions. Even as we move toward peace, I can't promise you absolute freedom from pain or total deliverance, at least not in the ways we might immediately desire. But I'll do my very best to chart a path through your thoughts and questions in productive, peace-giving ways.

What we will learn is how to abide in God when circumstances don't seem fair and when the plan doesn't make sense. We'll learn how to endure when our prayers seem to go unanswered and when it feels like the people we love most might not be with us in eternity.

I hope you will feel comforted and understood. Most of all, I hope you will know that you are not alone.

The road ahead is challenging. We need to allow room to process our grief. That's why, throughout these chapters, you'll find Reflection Rooms—places to practically apply the things we're discussing. In these Reflection Rooms, we'll recall Scripture, wrestle with questions, reframe our mindset, and request help from God. Here, I encourage you to take the time you need to fully engage and connect with God.

You'll also find a Prayer Starter at the end of every chapter to help open conversations with God about the things you're walking through. I recommend you pray these audibly, or perhaps use them to begin a prayer journal entry. He desires to meet you in your processing.

Finally, at the end of the book, you'll find a prayer of intercession for your friends and family. I hope this will be a tool you can use as you take the names of *your* loved ones to the Lord. Remember, He hears each and every name. He hears your pleading.

I'd like to mention one other point of information before we move forward. I'll talk about some close relationships in this book, and as you know, this book's subject is quite sensitive. That's why the people you'll read about here are composite characters, not actual individuals. I've even incorporated a few fictional elements. The nature of the interactions you'll see and the emotions I portray are very much unchanged from the actual events, but I love all my friends and family dearly, so I've gone to great lengths to protect their privacy and individual stories. I'm grateful for your understanding.

When I met my friend Charlotte, I didn't realize the journey of love and grief that would unfold or the questions about life, death, and eternity that would be brought to the surface—not just for Charlotte but for all the lost people I love. I am waiting for God to rescue so many loved ones.

This book is for everyone who has loved the lost. For everyone who has seen the beauty in their creation and marveled at the work of God's hand. It's for everyone who has desperately pleaded with, cried out to, and begged God to rescue their friends and family. For everyone who has thrown themselves at the foot of God's mercy seat and heard Him say, "Wait."

May you be filled with comfort, hope, and ultimately, peace, knowing that the God of the universe is in control and He is writing a redemptive story. Even more than you can imagine, God desires that you would have *peace in the waiting.*

Prayer Starter

Lord, thank You for Your abundant patience with me and my loved ones. Thank You for Your presence with me as I process my thoughts, questions, and emotions about the eternities of my friends and family. Please remind me of Your goodness, and let me experience Your divine comfort. Help me lay all my doubts, frustrations, and confusion at Your feet. In their place, give me hope in Your divine plan, and please gently guide me to peace in my waiting.

Part 1

The Thoughts
We Think

Chapter 1

This Situation Feels Unfair

In fifth grade, I won the red-and-black mountain bike in a school-wide raffle. On a flight home from vacation in college, I won the passenger grand prize giveaway: two hundred dollars. I've won holiday gift baskets at multiple office parties. I've won social media giveaways. I've never purchased a lottery ticket, but I've often thought I should give it a shot. I've always been a lucky person.

I feel much the same way when it comes to my faith. I had every advantage growing up. I was raised in a Christian household, went to church most Sundays, attended Sunday school and vacation Bible school, and had some degree of solid Christian community. I never had an overwhelmingly negative experience at church, and most of the religious folks I knew were genuine and well-meaning. Most of my extended family identified at least culturally as Christian, and what's more, I was raised in South Carolina, right in the middle of the Bible Belt.

In terms of external obstacles to faith, I've had very few. So I can get caught up on the fact that so many of my nonbelieving friends didn't have the same advantages I did. I often feel less chosen, more like I was entered into a cosmic birth lottery and hit the jackpot. Sometimes, it feels unfair to me, like I had a better shot than others. This thought keeps me up at night. Even more than the pain, confusion, doubt, and despair I feel about my loved ones' eternities, my own luck distresses me.

Maybe this thought has crossed your mind as well. I have friends who come from abusive homes, friends who grew up in families that followed different religions or none at all, and many friends whose backgrounds include some questionable church theology or even mistreatment by church congregations or leadership. It's no wonder that of the few of them who *have* realized the possibility of God's existence, even fewer have chosen to follow Him. Such a leap to faith would be great. And the odds of it happening just seem low.

I feel that even if I shared the gospel with these friends a thousand times over, their response would, at best, be, "That's nice." In fact, I'd go so far as to say I have done this. Perhaps not a thousand times, but definitely dozens. Still, the people I love go about their daily lives apart from Christ, terrifyingly unaware of what eternity could hold for them.

If you're anything like me, you read the accounts in the Bible of entire villages rejecting the gospel and Jesus's command for the disciples to leave those towns and shake the dust from their feet,[1] and you think to yourself, *What if people I love live in that town?* And you might wonder, *How could a God who crafted man in His image, ordaining each individual's personal existence, leave entire cities behind, shaking the dust from His feet on the way out?* If we were to stop here, we might say this all seems pretty unfair, if not cruel. Especially when our loved ones seem to be in that "village."

One night after sharing dinner at Charlotte's apartment, I was struck particularly hard by the realization that this person I adored continued to live her life separated from her Creator—and she didn't even know. No words of mine seemed to have an impact on her beliefs or even her curiosity. Walking to my car that evening, I couldn't stop thinking, *If she were to die today, she'd spend eternity in a place most of us don't like to think about, let alone discuss.* The unfairness of the situation seemed to wrap around my heart and constrict it.

Crying the entire way home, I let God know how confused I was. I let Him know how little sense it made that He'd created mankind only to let so many be consumed by the world, never learning to worship Him. I turned off the radio and the air conditioner, and I drove home with tears blurring the streetlights. It seemed to be a very cruel world, indeed. But as I cried out to the Lord, I felt the Spirit gently remind me that I was right—nothing in this world *is* entirely fair, and it never will be. This world, in many regards, is an experience in cruelty.

But there's good news too: God is not cruel. And He's certainly not unfair. In fact, He meets us in the unfairness we experience. He comforts us. He redeems our brokenness. He even sent His Son to die on the cross so that all the unfair, cruel realities of this life would eventually pass away. They're fading to dust, day by day. And one day, very soon, they will be no more.

Thanks to Jesus, all the suffering we don't understand now will be made clear in eternity. Our view of fairness might even be conformed to God's all-knowing perspective. One day, we won't have to wonder anymore. We won't drive home crying, afraid of what lies ahead for the people we love most.

I'm looking forward to that day ... but I don't live there yet.

Reflection Room

Wrestle: Are you ever tempted to view God as unfair or even cruel in this season of waiting? As we begin our journey, consider spending some time in the Psalms as you process your pain. See how the psalmists direct their sorrows back to God as a good Father, even when they are under debilitating distress. Reflect on their heart postures of worship and surrender. Remember the power and might of God described in Psalm 33, paying particular attention to verses 20–22:

> Our soul waits for the LORD;
>   he is our help and our shield.
> For our heart is glad in him,
>   because we trust in his holy name.
> Let your steadfast love, O LORD, be upon us,
>   even as we hope in you.

Some Things Are Not Ours to Know

Recently, I had a discussion with a wise mentor at my church. Her mother had passed away unexpectedly, leaving their family to grieve and grapple with unanswered questions. Despite a lifetime of service, prayer, and concern for her mother, my mentor doesn't know if her mother ever repented before Christ. As a result, she doesn't know where her mother resides in eternity. She doesn't know if she will ever see her mother again.

Deeply troubled, she turned to her husband with her questions, fears, and sorrow. He comforted her by sharing a sentiment that might help quiet your questioning heart as well: some things are not ours to know.

On the surface, this didn't feel like much of a comfort to me. But mulling it over, I realized that we all come to the Lord in the same way: by *faith*. And in faith, our hearts can be comforted in the knowledge that, while we don't know all things, our Father in heaven does. He knows all things and ordains all things in the context of His perfect, unceasing love. In our faith, we trust our Father. And who better to trust so wholly than a Father who sees all that we are and loves us completely in spite of ourselves?

I bet we've all received our fair share of well-intentioned comforting with reminders of God's omniscience and sovereignty. We can also be encouraged by Scripture. I'm reminded of Romans 8:28, in particular, which reads, "And we know that in all things God works for the good of those who love him, who have been called according to his purpose" (NIV).

I know, you've probably heard that a million times. But consider this: He doesn't just work in all *things*. He also works in the hearts of all people. He knows the state of our hearts: hardened or inclined to Him, willing to see Him or not. God made my friend Charlotte. It's even more comforting to meditate on the fact that He knows Charlotte better than I do. He's intimately familiar with her heart, and He knows the paths her life will take.

He doesn't just work in all things. He also works in the hearts of all people.

When I revisit my thoughts on the unfairness of life, I land on the same conclusion every time: when we expect *only* good things from the world—fairness, justice, peace, clarity—we're sure to be disappointed. This world is not fair. Shrouded in sin, the world is full of confusing, painful, unfair circumstances. Ironically, it is our own doing. Sin paves the way for worlds of pain. We ourselves are the inventors of the cruelty we experience.

When we try to reconcile our lives with how God intended for us to live before the fall of man in the garden of Eden, we'll be continually perplexed and dismayed. We can see remnants of that life, of course. We can enjoy the beauty of God's creation. We can revel in covenant signs like rainbows. We can experience God's love displayed through others. We can welcome all the wonderful emotions that we were created to experience—joy, excitement, amusement, awe, and peace, to name a few. We can appreciate God's artistry in our friends and family and neighbors. These beautiful parts of our design are shattered fragments of our intended lives lying all around us like broken mirror pieces reflecting back to us the glory of God.

But this world in all its brokenness, bearing the depravity and weight of sin, will never measure up. A wide expanse exists between this broken world and the new world to come. And so, when this world does not live up to our expectations, it's okay to mourn. We *should* mourn. But we can let it be our aim to mourn well, remembering that some things are not ours to know.

Reflection Room

Recall: Psalm 139:13–14 and reflect on how it applies to your loved ones. To whom do they belong? Be comforted in the knowledge that God knows your loved ones because He ordained their existence before time began. He formed them intricately out of His deep love.

> For you formed my inward parts;
>   you knitted me together in my mother's womb.
> I praise you, for I am fearfully and wonderfully
>   made.
>   Wonderful are your works;
>   my soul knows it very well.

Go Therefore and Make Disciples

Walking this journey of mourning feels acutely unfair because the eternal fate of people is something we were made to care deeply about.

We were created to be disciples of Christ, sharing God's love with others through the power of the Holy Spirit at work in our hearts. In Matthew 28:19, Jesus commands, "Go therefore and make disciples of all nations." When we start to take salvation personally, we're literally living out our global purpose as commissioned by God Himself. It's a call that demands our time, our resources, and our unique personalities.

I won't lie though—I haven't always thought of it that way. For much of my life, I've kept a busy calendar, running from one appointment to the next to fit in workouts, dinner with friends, social activities, work ... you name it. I've lived much of life so busy and distracted that even in sharing the gospel I never paused to consider that my friends, coworkers, and neighbors might be living and dying completely separated from God.

The pandemic changed all that.

For the first time, my schedule was cleared. My plans were canceled. My life seemed rather empty. I still had lots of friends and a wide social circle, but the entire world was on lockdown for a while, and everything came to a crashing stop. As people were dying of the COVID-19 virus, I opened my eyes to the quickly coming eternity and began to seriously consider what might happen to the people I loved if nothing changed.

In the quietness of my home, I was struck deeply with concern for their souls. Don't get me wrong. I'd shared the gospel with good intentions and hope in my heart, and I'd been troubled by the world's separation from its Maker. But this time, the observation was accompanied by a deeper burden and heaviness than in the past. Where previously I'd cared and then moved on to the next obligation on my schedule, now I sat in silence before the Lord until my care grew into deep and paralyzing sorrow.

In solitude, I wasn't quite sure what to do with all that grief.

If you're anything like me, you may have grappled with that sorrow too, especially as we were forced to face the constant threat of death on a global scale. Questions about the eternal lives of people I didn't even know weighed heavily on me. Where were all these people going?

I was caught off guard at first. I would describe my newfound awareness as sort of an encompassing darkness for which there seemed to be no immediate light. I became deeply confused and frustrated by the unfairness I perceived. But then I realized that these negative emotions were never part of God's original design. I certainly hadn't read about confusion and frustration *before* the fall of man.

As I began to go before the Lord in search of answers and comfort, He reminded me in His Word to approach Him in faith because faith, when exercised, grows.

Things *weren't* fair. Things weren't as they *should* be. I began to realize that my feelings of unfairness stemmed from my unmet expectations. None of this was what I would choose. My mission to go and make disciples felt extraordinarily difficult, and I felt like I was being set up for failure. I had a whole laundry list of complaints. I needed to figure out what to do with all my angst. As I began to go before the Lord in search of answers and comfort, He reminded me in His Word to approach Him in faith because faith, when exercised, *grows.*

Hebrews 4:15–16 is one such reminder. We can bring our needs before God and trust that He will meet us with His mercy.

> For we do not have a high priest who is unable to sympathize with our weaknesses, but one who in every respect has been tempted as we are, yet without sin. Let us then with confidence draw near to the throne of grace, that we may receive mercy and find grace to help in time of need.

He comforted me with gentle, tenderhearted mercy. It soon became clear that before I could move forward, I needed to lament over the fact that the people I loved most had not come to know their Father in heaven or to understand His love for them. I felt acutely aware of their separation and of the difficulty of the mission set before me.

Lament is a concept we see in Scripture. When we experience suffering or loss, we feel pain. But rather than absorbing our grief or sorrow, letting those feelings infiltrate our attitudes and outlook, we can take our pain to God in lament.

In the Word, we see psalmists lament their distress, calling out to God for deliverance. In the book of Job, we read about Job's suffering and his expressions of lament to the Lord as he seeks understanding for his circumstances. And in Romans 9, we even see examples of lament over the spiritual condition of other people (vv. 1–4). Scripture is full of lamentation.

Our lament is for our loved ones. We want them to experience salvation, much in the way Paul describes Christ in Colossians 1:19–23:

For in him all the fullness of God was pleased to dwell, and through him to reconcile to himself all things, whether on earth or in heaven, making peace by the blood of his cross.

And you, who once were alienated and hostile in mind, doing evil deeds, he has now reconciled in his body of flesh by his death, in order to present you holy and blameless and above reproach before him, if indeed you continue in the faith, stable and steadfast, not shifting from the hope of the gospel that you heard, which has been proclaimed in all creation under heaven, and of which I, Paul, became a minister.

Here, Paul makes it clear: We have been separated from God by our sin against Him. We've directed our love not to God but to idols, whether those are ourselves or things in the world. We all deserve His just judgment. He is perfect, and in our brokenness, we cannot stand before Him.

But the gospel changes everything. The gospel message is this: Though we have turned from God, He has pursued us. He came to us in the person of Christ, whose sacrifice on the cross paid the price for our sin. Through faith in Christ, we can be reconciled to the Lord.

Salvation comes when we put our faith in these truths and their source—Jesus. I want my loved ones to follow Him and to live for His glory. I want them to place their faith in Christ and be restored to our Father by His grace alone. I want them to walk in the truth of Titus 2:11–14:

> For the grace of God has appeared, bringing salvation
> for all people, training us to renounce ungodliness
> and worldly passions, and to live self-controlled,
> upright, and godly lives in the present age, waiting
> for our blessed hope, the appearing of the glory of
> our great God and Savior Jesus Christ, who gave
> himself for us to redeem us from all lawlessness and
> to purify for himself a people for his own possession
> who are zealous for good works.

Bearing in mind our Great Commission, we know that the desire we carry for the salvation of our loved ones is inherently good. What we're grieving is the difference between the good things we long for and the confusing reality we observe. Before we dive into our peace-seeking journey, we can acknowledge our frustration and pain.

There's one more thing we might need to acknowledge before we move forward on this journey together. I'm confident that, as Bible-believing Christians, we all believe the gospel message we've just walked through. And yet, even *we* may have differing convictions on some matters of Scripture. We're talking about a deeply personal, deeply painful topic. It is possible that you and I might come to this message with differing perspectives or interpretations. Believers across the centuries have approached the dynamics of God's will and human free will from different perspectives, especially as they pertain to salvation.

I'd like you to feel very welcome here, wherever you stand and whatever you've experienced. As you read this book, please take what is helpful and feel free to leave the rest. My struggles might not be your struggles. And we may not align on every thought or question or interpretation I present. But as Bible-believing Christians, we have the divine privilege of bearing with one another in love despite any unique convictions we might bring to the table.

I wish I could share a cup of tea with you and listen to your concerns and questions and understand the ways you process those things through your unique lens. I wish I could learn about the journey that led you to this book and pray with you for all the lost people you love. I am so thankful that we are united in the message of the gospel. I'm confident that we have more things in common than we have differences. And if we ever do get to meet, I promise to be quick to listen.

So if I present any individual viewpoints through these pages that don't align with your understanding or with your struggle, I encourage you to converse with mature believers in your life and carry one another's burdens as you seek to find peace in your waiting. I encourage you to stand firm in your convictions and to be curious, to listen long, and to love well. And I ask humbly for your abundant grace.

My desire in discussing such a deeply personal challenge is to live out the apostle Paul's command found in Ephesians 4:

> I therefore, a prisoner for the Lord, urge you to walk in a manner worthy of the calling to which you have been called, with all humility and gentleness, with patience, bearing with one another in

love, eager to maintain the unity of the Spirit in the
bond of peace. (vv. 1–3)

It is so appropriate that this passage of Scripture concludes with
the idea of peace—and not only peace but our "bond of peace." I
hope that we can walk in peace together. But know that I desire to
point you not to me, my words, or my understanding as your source
of peace but only to Christ.

Division over the interpretations of Bible-believing brothers
and sisters is another thing I often pause and lament on this side of
heaven. Division is brutal. We're here together because we mourn
being divided from people we love over the most important thing in
the entire world: the gospel. We know Christ, and the people we love
do not. If we're not careful, even mourning this divide can lead us
to focus on ourselves rather than on Jesus and all He came to offer.

So, as we practice lament over unmet expectations and unfairness in any area of life, we should take care not to sink into self-pity.
When we refuse joy, we invite steady streams of sorrow. I know
because I experienced it! My despair over my lost friends became soul
crushing. Isolating. It did not reap hope.

In time, I have learned to grieve in a way that promotes healing:
by taking all that pain and bringing it before the Lord in lament.
Our Father in heaven is eager to show us His gentle loving-kindness,
to listen to our hurting hearts, and to fill us with steadfast hope. But
before we can *make* progress, we must be willing to *seek* it.

I encourage you to open that line of communication with the
Lord and give Him your life as a stage upon which to present His
grace.

Reflection Room

Request: Lord, thank You for the deep care You've given me for the lost. Please give me the strength to bring You my lament. Even as I experience the unfairness in the world, let me also experience Your merciful loving-kindness. Let my pain not keep me from You but instead keep me running to You.

Let My Heart Be Tender

As my months of prayer for Charlotte continued, my heart began to harden. I even began to avoid time with God. Rarely have I been more miserable. I came to realize that a *heart with tough walls around it has a very hard time letting in joy*. In many ways, this hardening carried into my relationships as well.

I became impatient. I felt less empathy. I didn't have a lot of space to give to the problems of others. My own suffering kept me from showing up well in the lives of the people I loved. I was so focused on my own pain that I couldn't see the struggles of others. A stubborn heart replaced my servant's heart, as I punished myself through an unwillingness to rely humbly on God.

In these prolonged times, there was one plea that would eventually pull me back into a place of trust. That plea was a cry to God to let my heart be tender. My prayer journal captures me begging God on more than one occasion to give me back my tenderness, to end the cycles of misery, and to let the pain coexist with the joy He wants us all to experience.

When we're left to our own devices, pain has the capacity to overwhelm us and blind us to God's goodness. That unchecked pain can suffocate our trust in God. It can distract us from the mission He has set before us. It can cause us to grow weary.

In moments of irritation, we can listen to the Lord speak gently to us from His Word. Psalm 16:5–6 reminds us:

> The LORD is my chosen portion and my cup;
>   you hold my lot.
> The lines have fallen for me in pleasant places;
>   indeed, I have a beautiful inheritance.

When we're tempted to dwell on unfairness, this psalm reminds us that the Lord has foreseen our circumstances and has always been present, leading us through even the situations that seem the most unjust. Our relationships, our struggles, our pain ... they aren't surprises to Him. Our Father has placed good boundary lines around our lives. He's using the things that seem unfair to us to draw us closer to Him. He's using our painful moments to refine us and sanctify us. The boundary lines don't separate or punish us, but rather, they lead us back to the Father.

Though religious events weren't common in her life growing up, Charlotte would occasionally attend church with relatives. From the way I understand it, this proved to be more harmful than helpful. Church messages delivered more promises of hell than of hope. But for a time, as a child, Charlotte did consider the existence of a higher power that might, for some people, be called God. She told me, though, that the most plausible version of a god she could come up with was nothing more than an apathetic creator who'd made the earth, populated it with people, and then sat idly by, watching from a distance and leaving the creations to their own devices, come what may.

You and I have the divine privilege of knowing that nothing could be further from the truth. Our God is intimately involved in the details. He sees our friends and family, and He pursues them. He sees our confusion, and He wants to comfort us. That doesn't mean He'll give us all the answers. Some things are simply not ours to know. But rest assured that God is not limited by the unfairness we perceive in the world. He operates in a plane that exists above brokenness. None of us are outside His reach.

When we're left to our own devices, pain has the capacity to overwhelm us and blind us to God's goodness.

I might've once thought myself lucky, but in matters of salvation, luck's got nothing to do with it. God isn't pulling names out of His hat in a cosmic raffle. He sees all people, and He knows all hearts. He loves our sweet friends and family ten thousand times more than we can possibly imagine. He is totally unlimited by human standards of fairness or chance. Rest in the Lord's great love and know that His plan is not at all random. Rather, it is based on a great knowing, not only of the end result but also of the details in between.

Prayer Starter

Thank You, Father, for the ways that You are mindful of my friends and family. You hold their lives in Your hands, and You love them deeply. When circumstances feel acutely unfair to me, I am even more thankful that my view is incomplete and limited. Please be gentle with me in my confusion and pain. Please let my heart not be hardened by frustration or impatience. Let me bring my hurt to You rather than filling my mind and schedule with distractions. Please keep my heart tender and allow me to receive the comfort and joy that You have for me even in the waiting.

Chapter 2

I'm Frustrated with My Loved Ones

Charlotte's father walked out of her life when she was young. Her mom worked two jobs to provide for Charlotte and her sister. Her childhood was challenging, to say the least. There's a lot of lingering resentment there. In my discussions with Charlotte about faith, we often reach a crossroads when we arrive at the concept of God as a Father.

"I know what fathers do," Charlotte says. "They leave."

She still sees her dad occasionally, but tension remains. It's a deep wound. They've talked about what happened and why, and he longs to be part of her life. He's aged into a gentle, dependable person. He lives nearby, and he's reconciled with Charlotte's mom. They even exchange holiday and birthday messages. He desires reconciliation with Charlotte too. She wants that, but she struggles to forgive him. No amount of repentance or consistency is enough.

Having grown up in a split family myself, I can understand her feelings. But I so deeply desire her to know that her heavenly Father will never leave or forsake her (Deut. 31:8). I also long for her to find peace with her earthly dad—to view him the way God sees him: as a sinner in need of grace.

Restoring broken relationships is hard work, and it might not always be possible. But I like to imagine a world in which God's grace and forgiveness in Charlotte's life pave the way for her to offer grace and forgiveness to her dad. I don't really know how it would play out. But I do know the gospel offers unprecedented mercy and divine forgiveness. The gospel presents us with a perfect, present, consistent, reliable Father who doesn't leave. I like to imagine a world in which Charlotte knows Him personally.

Do you ever imagine this kind of outcome for your loved ones? When my imagination takes over, I see ideal salvation scenarios all planned out—and the waves of healing that follow.

If only they would believe, then:

- They'd be able to rid themselves of that habit or addiction.
- They'd be able to forgive and move past that hurt.
- They'd be able to overcome that crippling anxiety.
- They'd find an eternal, perfect Father who will never walk away.
- They'd become part of a loving body of Christ that would support and uphold them through struggles and pain.

Sometimes my imagination ventures so far as to make it about myself.

If only they would believe, then:

- They would know that what I believe isn't foolish.
- Our relationship would be so much easier.
- They wouldn't be so selfish or difficult.
- They would finally understand me.
- Their eternity would stop causing me so, so much grief.
- Things could finally be different—for all of us.

It's tempting to think of salvation as a quick solution rather than a divinely timed journey of repentance, sanctification, and surrender. And even an intimate relationship with Christ won't resolve every worldly problem or change every challenging circumstance, especially right away.

It will, of course, resolve our loved ones' ultimate problem—separation from Christ for all eternity. But what do we do in the meantime?

As I've waited for my loved ones to follow Christ, I admit I've succumbed to some frustration. Mainly, I'm frustrated with the situation. But sometimes, I find myself becoming impatient with these people I'm waiting for. I'd like to go ahead and skip to the happy ending.

Whether they realize it or not, by failing to submit to the Lord, our lost loved ones are operating as their own gods. A hard truth to reckon with is that we all constantly worship. Our lives all point to the power of someone or something. Our lost loved ones' worlds revolve around themselves, and why wouldn't they? There's nothing else out there, after all, at least not in their minds. *They* are the center of their stories.

They think they're the main character in a universe where every man must fend for himself. They don't realize that Jesus is the lead character in the story of the world.

These are well-meaning people, people who love me and whom I love dearly. By the world's standards, these friends and family members are kind and charismatic and "good." They give to charity. They volunteer at service events. They drive their friends to the airport. But what they don't realize is that they're assuming the wrong role in the production. They think they're the main character in a universe where every man must fend for himself.

They don't realize that Jesus is the lead character in the story of the world. The universe revolves around, for, and through Him.

If you have close friendships with nonbelievers, I'm sure you understand what I'm getting at. It's not that these friends are selfish. Describing them that way would be painting them with too broad a brush. No. It's more that their sense of self is excessively inflated.

This makes perfect sense because, in the absence of an omnipotent creator, what would hold more power than our individual souls? In a world of random and meaningless creation, what would be more worthy than humans?

But this attitude, when lived out over time, can make people extraordinarily self-focused. This becomes all the more true in an individualistic society that prizes reputation and personal glory. These hearts, when not submitted to God, serve only themselves.

Reflection Room

Wrestle: Are you experiencing frustration over improvements you believe would take place in the lives of your loved ones if only they would repent and follow Jesus? How might you bring those frustrations before the Lord, choosing instead to direct your mental energy to His unlimited creativity and grace for their lives? Reflect on Isaiah 45:9. Remember that the Lord is the Maker, and He will shape His creation in His time: ✳

> Woe to him who strives with him who formed him,
>   a pot among earthen pots!
> Does the clay say to him who forms it, "What are
>   you making?"
>   or "Your work has no handles"?

Gaze on Things Unseen

My observations of our sense of self have led me to notice a big gap. It's a gap I experience without exception whenever I consider my close relationships with the lost people I love. Because they do not yet have new hearts in Christ, they do not have the hearts of servants. In other words, the Spirit does not dwell within them.

A friend of mine named Jessie used to live near me. She's since moved, but back then, we'd take long walks together around our city, appreciating the monuments, photographing the cherry blossoms, and pretending to be tourists. Being neighbors, we were uniquely qualified to meet each other's needs—late-night meal ingredients, laundry emergencies, spare-key services ... that sort of thing.

After a few years of friendship, I noticed that the level of care we offered each other wasn't quite even. I'll admit I developed some bitterness over the lack of reciprocation. I had started keeping score. This didn't seem like the right attitude for me to adopt, especially since I was trying to share my faith with Jessie. I was one of the only Christians she knew. I just wanted to love her well.

So I began to pray about my attitude.

My bitterness was hurting me, and it certainly wasn't helping Jessie. If anything, my resentment stood in opposition to God's love and was becoming an obstacle to the work He wanted to do through me. Ironically, I was displaying the same self-focus that upset me in others.

Over time, the Lord showed me that I had been hoping in the wrong things. My intentions were good: I wanted to see my friend be saved and her life be conformed to Christ. But my expectations were wrong, so I was constantly disappointed by what I deemed to be bad behavior on her part. Namely, the lack of reciprocal care.

In this case, I'm not speaking about boundaries or codependency, concerns best worked through with a knowledgeable counselor. I was serving Jessie in a reasonable measure, and she was a kind, gentle friend. My problem was my focus. I was frustrated with Jessie because I'd made the situation all about me.

That's when I realized that the Lord didn't want me keeping score, nor did He want me focused on perfecting Jessie's behavior. Instead,

He wanted my focus to rest only on Him. He wanted me to know that the power to change Jessie resides not with me or even with Jessie but only with Him. I was, as 2 Corinthians 4:18 tells me, to set my gaze not on things seen but rather on things unseen.

Reflection Room

Request: Lord, please search my heart and root out resentment. Convict me of my own self-focus. Please forgive me for the ways in which I've kept score. I believe following Jesus inevitably leads to growth, and I deeply desire to see heart change in the lives of my loved ones. But help me also be continually refined by Your pruning. Shine Your light on the areas of sin and selfishness in my life, that I might grow to look more like Christ.

Expectations and Eternal Heritage

We can shift our focus from the behavior we observe to God's transformative power when we realize one thing: despite our desires for heart change in the lives of our friends and family, we cannot expect nonbelievers to behave like those who are saved.

Why would the hearts and attitudes of the lost ever align with hearts that are truly made new in Christ? When we walk into any human relationship and expect perfect, godly treatment, we will always be disappointed. But this proves especially true when we love those who do not follow Jesus. Our friends and family may be kind, decent people who are polite and charitably inclined, but they're still unsaved.

Despite our desires for heart change in the lives of our friends and family, we cannot expect nonbelievers to behave like those who are saved.

They're not worse sinners than anyone else, though. Paul tells us in Romans 3:10–12, "None is righteous, no, not one; no one understands; no one seeks for God. All have turned aside; together they have become worthless; no one does good, not even one."

So the disappointment we experience doesn't come from anyone's inherent goodness or badness. We're all inherently bad.

However, as Christians, our lives and hearts are pointed heavenward. By God's total grace, we are given new hearts. As we grow in Christ, submit to His will, and are sanctified through His Spirit at work within us, our paths will simply diverge from those whose lives are oriented toward their own earthly glory rather than God's eternal glory.

The Spirit's transformational power enables us:

- to be conformed to Christ (2 Cor. 3:17–18)
- to fight against sin and strongholds in our lives (John 16:8)

- to understand and apply God's Word (John 14:26; 16:13–15)
- to seek unity within the church (Eph. 4:1–6)
- to walk in the fruit of the Spirit (Gal. 5:22–25)

This doesn't mean we should avoid relationships with lost people. We're on this journey together *because of* the depth of our love for our unsaved family and friends. But no man or woman will ever have the power to fill us up or meet the whole of our emotional and relational needs.

Attempting to satisfy ourselves with created things carves out an urn in our hearts that will be filled not with contentment but with the ashes of disappointment and grief. Only the Lord is capable of satisfying us completely.

I've learned that, while I don't need my loved ones or their perfect treatment to fill me up or edify me all the time, I do desire that our hearts be united in our eternal heritage.

God designed us to live in biblical community and to pursue unity within the church. He gave us the Spirit to do so. So, naturally, we desire that our lost friends and family will join us on our journey. We want them pointed in the same direction. We desire for them to share in the knowledge of the meaning of life itself. The truth of the gospel is, in a word, foundational.

So it's not hard to understand why we grow weary in waiting. It's exhausting to see the people we love find their treasure in idols. But we must fight against becoming weary in our affection for them. Pray against resentment and bitterness. And make no mistake, this *is* a spiritual battle.

As we adjust our expectations and direct our focus to God, let's also remember to find our fullness in Him. Rather than finding hope in the perfect behavior of man, we can hope in the God whose Spirit can redeem all who are broken.

Reflection Room

Reframe: Instead of focusing on salvation as a solution for all the problems of life, take your thoughts captive and dwell on the Father and the trustworthy mysteries of His work. Rather than creating plans, direct your mental energy to cultivating patience. What are some of the unexpected ways you've seen God transform lives by the power of His Spirit?

If Only They Would Believe

I've been praying for a few loved ones for years. Still, I see the same negative behavior patterns in their lives. I see their dissatisfaction and their anxieties, their addictions and their obsessions. And to be honest, it's hard for me to fathom how they make it through their day. They must be mentally stronger than I am, because if I couldn't cast my cares on the Lord (however imperfect I am at this), I'm not sure how I would carry on through seemingly impossible circumstances. But despite their continual (and usually outwardly strong) trudging, I catch occasional glimpses of their internal struggle. That's the frustrating part for me. I love them. I want freedom for them. *If only* they would believe.

Now, it's important for me to emphasize that this book does not attempt to address toxic, abusive, or otherwise unhealthy relationships from which there are biblically valid reasons to depart. This book speaks about lost people in our lives whom we love and with whom we have healthy relationships (and, occasionally, *healthy* amounts of conflict).

Apart from those exceptions, know that you're not in the wrong place loving the wrong people at the wrong time. The Lord brings people together on purpose, some in whom we sow seeds, some whom we cultivate, some with whom we get the joy of experiencing the harvest, some simply to bless, and some who even provide for *us*.

We are free to love our lost friends so that our words and actions might be edifying to them, to us, and ultimately to God and so that the love of Christ might shine through us.

Believer, your life path has been aligned with your lost people. Your lives crossing is no accident, and God is not surprised by your meeting. The stories of your lives are beautifully woven together by the Maker. We are free to love our lost friends so that our words and actions might be edifying to them, to us, and ultimately to God and so that the love of Christ might shine through us.

We don't, however, have grounds to expect that their behavior will begin to look drastically different, apart from true heart change through Christ. Even where you may see positive change in character, be careful not to place your hope in behavioral shifts alone.

In my brief period of bitterness toward Jessie, I tried to change our relationship's dynamics so that I would feel more considered and cared for. We had some challenging conversations. Clear communication isn't a bad thing. It's good to have open, respectful dialogue. But even when I felt heard and considered in our friendship, Jessie's heart was no more inclined to God.

Anyone can make positive changes by pursuing wellness, giving up bad habits, walking away from unhealthy relationships, or treating others better. And we can root for these changes in others as well. But ultimately, these "steps in the right direction" do not provide sanctification, much less salvation.

Focusing too heavily on behavioral changes was a trap I fell into time and time again.

We should not hope that by helping someone choose better behavior that their soul will then be led in the "right direction." Instead, we should be watchful and prayerful, attentive to the Spirit, praying for God to lead them where He knows they need to be. Even our best efforts cannot change hearts, minds, or character apart from the Spirit.

We can certainly promote positive life change with love and encouragement. *But we cannot fix the areas of sin in the lives of our loved ones in order to achieve their salvation.* Sanctification does not lead to salvation. Sanctification begins after salvation.

Life after salvation is not a checklist; neither is the process by which a lost heart is saved. Sometimes with Jessie, I pushed a bit too hard. I acted as though God might see her "goodness" and deem her ready for His Spirit. I got caught up in using excessive amounts of energy to try to change my friend's heart and behavior apart from Christ.

When we choose to follow Jesus and we receive the gift of His Spirit, we're strengthened in our fight against sin. Thus, sin may offend a righteous heart. This is good. In fact, this helps us search for, recognize, and repent of our *own* sin. But God wants us to know that other people's sin, eternal direction, and life foundations are not our responsibility to manage or correct. In taking on the responsibility for changing hearts, God frees us to simply show up and love people without placing behavioral expectations on their shoulders. In releasing the reins, we become free to love all people without frustration, offense, or bitterness.

Reflection Room

Wrestle:

1. In what ways might you be too focused on fixing problems or viewing people as projects?
2. Are there any active relationships in which you might carefully consider and pray over your motivations?

3. Are you approaching any relationships in your life
   with expectations for sanctification achieved apart
   from the Spirit?

I Am Not God

Admittedly, my life as a believer is far from perfect. I struggle daily. I fall back into selfish tendencies, and I live in the same difficult world as everyone else, experiencing the same less-than-ideal circumstances we all face every day.

But because of Christ, the Spirit is always at work inside me, gently steering me back on course when I wander outside those boundary lines. I find peace in knowing my cares in this world are temporal because I follow a leader who is not me. *I am not my god.*

The thing is, when God isn't guiding our lives, an Enemy is. An Enemy who does not intend all things for our good but who roots for our destruction.

I shudder at the thought that, by refusing to submit their lives to God, so many people have no protection against this evil force, whether they realize it or not. Apart from God, the lost people I love are living in a world that intends them only harm.

One evening, I reflected fretfully over the horror of a world leader who seeks for death and destruction. The Lord comforted me, gently reminding me that even unbeknownst to my friends, He is still in control. The world apart from God *does* intend to harm them, but Genesis 50:20 reminds us that where harm is intended, the Lord can use it for good to accomplish His purposes: "You intended to harm me, but God intended it for good to accomplish what is now being done, the saving of many lives" (NIV).

> *In taking on the responsibility for changing hearts, God frees us to simply show up and love people without placing behavioral expectations on their shoulders.*

Despite the state of lost hearts, the sin and destruction in their lives, and the evil intent of the Enemy they are subject to, God is still good. He can still turn things around. And what's more, He knew all the things we now observe about our friends and family before the beginning of time. He knew about their trauma and addictions and selfishness. He knew about their difficult circumstances and failed relationships and broken careers. He knew about all the problems they would ever encounter and the hard things they would walk through. God is not surprised by their struggles or even by their unbelief. He saw it coming, for a really, really, really long time.

And there's more good news beyond God's omniscience. In His great power and artistry, He is capable of using any and all circumstances to draw our loved ones to Him. He is unlimited in His power and His merciful loving-kindness. Rest assured that He is in control of hearts that do not yet know Him. Hard circumstances are tools in His hand.

The world might intend to harm them, but God intends to use *all* things for good, to accomplish His purposes in and through them. Where we alone are not able, God is able. Where we cannot, God can.

Reflection Room

Recall: 1 Corinthians 13:12, which reminds us that while our vision is blurry, God fully sees everyone's storyline and fully knows all His image bearers: "For now we see in a mirror dimly, but then face to face. Now I know in part; then I shall know fully, even as I have been fully known."

Search My Heart

It's easy to plan perfect outcomes and solutions in our mind's eye. I know. I used to do it all the time. We ultimately want our friends to know God. To follow Jesus. To make Him the center of their lives. But in my moments of bitterness and irritation with God's timeline, I'm tempted to do the exact opposite. Ironically, I exercise the very behavior I want my friends to turn from: I trust in myself more than in God.

But God has woven the tapestry of humanity. The threads running through it are all interconnected with perfect precision, no thread sewn a moment before its time.

We are not the weavers. While we wait, we can set our sights on the same goal we have for lost people: to make God the center of our lives.

Earlier, we talked about the mental exhaustion and weariness that come from watching lost people continue to lead lives pointed in directions different from our own. And we talked about fighting against this burnout. Some of the heaviness we feel may also come from all the wrong ways we're expending our energy. Our planning. Our scheming. Our worrying.

If we can take our thoughts captive and submit their heaviness to God, He will replace our struggles with a far lighter burden. The answer is prayer.

God will deal gently with us, if only we reach out and ask Him. In the most desperate times of wanting to "fix" the lives of the people I love, I've asked God to save my friends and take away my feeling of personal culpability. And then I've asked Him this: "Father, I am hurting. Would You please deal gently with me?"

Let's consider praying not only that others will find salvation but also that God will search and purify the motives of our hearts. As the psalmist writes in Psalm 26:2:

> Prove me, O LORD, and try me;
> test my heart and my mind.

Prayer Starter

Father, thank You for carving a path on which my life intersected with the lives of the people I love. Thank You for the rich blessing of knowing them. Thank You for writing our stories in a way that is good and glorifying. Protect me from disappointment when the lives of my lost friends and family don't play out the way I would like. Please protect my heart from bitterness against them and especially against You, as this hurts me and those I love. Please meet me in my weariness and uphold me. And please do not allow me or my attitude to stand in the way as You seek them.

Chapter 3

My Hope Is Slipping Away

I'm an extremely picky eater. Venturing much beyond bread and cheese is a big win.

Sure—some of it has to do with taste. But honestly, I'm often intimidated by appearance too.

I remember the first time I saw gnocchi. *That is not okay*, I thought. Have you ever *really* looked at gnocchi? It's disturbingly close in appearance to some kind of larvae. And some of it is covered in *green stuff*. I wanted to run away.

Left to myself, I never would've gone anywhere near it, but one night, I found myself trapped. A friend invited me over for dinner, and the meal had already been prepared. Guess what it was?

With terror in my heart, I took my first bite.

My world was changed. This was the best food I had ever tasted. How could something that looked so bad actually be so good? It didn't make sense! Relying on what I could observe, I would've gone on assuming the worst for my entire life. I would've missed out on something so good sitting right in front of me. I assumed that what I saw represented a reality that I'd already decided on. It didn't look good, so it couldn't be good.

We're so keen to rely on what we see. I wonder how many other foods I've missed out on (but please don't give my friends any ideas—you can never go wrong with cheese). My hope so often depends on what I see as well. Does the situation *look* good? Does it look like anything might change? We're no fools. If it doesn't look good, why would we call it good?

But here's the thing: The moments I rely the most on my own sight correspond perfectly with the moments I doubt the most. My sight excludes God's mystery.

We don't need to trust in what we see. We can trust in the One who sees everything. ✳

Does doubt creep into your life unexpectedly? You're doing your best to take it one day at a time, but at some point, you look up and realize you're no longer expecting to see God's goodness in the lives of your loved ones. Sometimes, this doubt sneaks up on me. I don't even realize I'm looking only to what I see. I ride waves of hope. I submit my desires to God. In my human nature, though, the waves do occasionally crash over my head. Discouragement overwhelms me, and I wonder, *Is it too late for them? Will they ever believe? Is all my hope for nothing?*

The truth is, I can't possibly know the answers to these questions. How *could* I know? I'm not God. So, upon deeper reflection, it seems the real issue here isn't that I don't *know* ... it's that I don't *believe.*

As much as I want to believe, as much as I cry out to the Lord to help my unbelief, some days I just don't see how change is possible, especially on the timeline that I would prefer. I believe the gospel, of course, but in these moments, I find myself lacking belief in God's perfect goodness when it comes to the lives of lost people I love.

The questions swirl in my mind, a hurricane of confusion: *Would their salvation not be a service to the kingdom of God? How could salvation on my immediate timeline ever be a bad thing? And if their salvation would always be good, why does the Lord seemingly delay answering my prayers on behalf of my friends? Why is He holding out on them?*

It's not just that I don't believe; it's that I'm frustrated by my lack of understanding. There is so much we cannot understand. But the unknown, when not surrendered to God, leads to doubt.

I hope pondering these questions won't make you doubt more. Know that I have asked every variation of every question in the doubter's playbook. And they've all led me back to the same place: Jesus.

Consider Jesus's remarks in the middle of the Last Supper as described in John 13. Jesus is eating with the disciples when He gets up, takes off His outer layer of clothing, wraps a towel around His waist, and begins to wash the disciples' feet. It's a bit of a bizarre scene, to be sure, particularly because the disciples are unaware of the events to come later that evening. Jesus knows what's going on, of course. But Peter asks, in what I assume was a puzzled and indignant tone, "Lord, are you going to wash my feet?" (v. 6 NIV).

And instead of responding with a simple affirmative answer or explanation, Jesus replies, "You do not realize now what I am doing, but later you will understand" (v. 7 NIV). Upon hearing this, Peter relents in submission.

After finishing His task, Jesus does explain why He washed the disciples' feet. But at first, He only asks them to submit. For Peter, at least, this submission comes with feelings of embarrassment, confusion, and even pride, as he can't understand why this is happening. If he had been in control, he wouldn't, in his human understanding, have allowed things to play out that way. It didn't make sense! He doubted the Lord's plan.

Even in this small occurrence, I share Peter's feelings. In considering my friend Charlotte's eternity, I display pride by expecting her to be saved right now, on my timeline. I experience deep confusion about why things have to be this way. I doubt God, as Peter did, because of my lack of understanding.

In deep thought over these feelings one evening, I felt led to Jesus's response to Peter in John 13:7, "You do not realize now what I am doing" (NIV). The Lord knows we don't understand. He knows we are hurting and confused. But He's assured us that we don't need to know all the details right now. He has a plan and a purpose. He knows everything that's going down this evening and a million years into the future. *We don't need to trust in what we see. We can trust in the One who sees everything.*

Reflection Room

Wrestle: In waiting for the salvation of lost people you love, have you noticed that lack of understanding contributes to a lack of trust in God? How might you restore that trust? Consider meditating on and praying through Psalm 28. The psalmist writes in Psalm 28:7:

> The LORD is my strength and my shield;
>   my heart trusts in him, and he helps me.
> My heart leaps for joy,
>   and with my song I praise him. (NIV)

Happily Ever After

On one particularly dark day, I wanted some encouragement, so I considered watching one of the many Christian fiction movies on my streaming services.

As I pondered my options, I became exasperated. On-screen, the story would surely culminate in the perfect, miraculous ending. Sometimes these hope-filled movies encourage my faith. But sometimes they take on a life of their own, demonstrating our ideal human solutions to problems here on earth. They represent the way we think things *should* be: the cancer is cured, the relationship is mended, and all the lost people are saved, turning their lives around and serving God's kingdom faithfully.

But in reality, such a "happily ever after" had evaded me. Even if I did live to see the salvation of my friends and family, it wouldn't play out within the two or so hours represented in the lives of fictional characters. I'd already been waiting years!

Of course, even in their fictional world, miracles don't happen overnight. Captions or time lapses often indicate that days, weeks, or months have passed in these characters' lives, and yet the characters remain so faithful, so prayerfully patient. The story is so, so ... clean.

Reality isn't clean. It's messy and full of struggle, full of tears and deep pain. If they ever made a feature film about my last few years of waiting, its box office sales would plummet well below historical lows. Scene after scene would depict me on my knees crying out to God. It definitely wouldn't have a perfect ending. At the time of writing this book, I still haven't seen any of my lost loved ones choose to follow Christ. If you're thinking, *Me neither*, then know, dear friend, that you are not alone. My heart breaks with yours.

Still, we hope for a miracle. And that's good, as long as we hope more in the Miracle Giver than in the miracle itself. Otherwise, we set ourselves up for disappointment if reality doesn't align with our expectations.

In other words:

- Hope for miracles, but hope even more in the good plans and perfect timing of God.

- Base your hope on the nature and character of God rather than on the things He can do to relieve your suffering right now.
- Hope in who He is rather than in the picture-perfect happy ending you desire.

Remember that His ending will be perfectly designed by Him. That is His very nature.

In Luke 11, Jesus tells a crowd, "Your eye is the lamp of your body. When your eyes are healthy, your whole body also is full of light. But when they are unhealthy, your body also is full of darkness. See to it, then, that the light within you is not darkness" (vv. 34–35 NIV).

He's trying to explain to the people of that day that rather than relying on "signs," they just need healthy eyes—proper motives and right heart attitudes—to experience the light of Christ.

The message remains true today. When we set our eyes properly on Christ, we can be filled with His light, hoping in the truth of salvation. We can take joy in what is lasting. But when we are looking for "signs" (like a change in circumstance or miraculous provision), we are looking to the wrong things.

I found myself secretly basing my assessment of God's goodness on His provision of good things.

After revisiting this chapter of Luke, I shifted my perspective. I realized that rather than hoping in Christ Himself, I'd been hoping in the things He could do for me. I was frustrated because He had not given me proof on my terms. I was demanding a response from a God who had already told me all I needed to do was trust Him.

I love the English Standard Version of Luke 11:35, which says, "Therefore be careful lest the light in you be darkness."

My world had indeed become dark because rather than filling myself with the light of Christ, I'd filled myself with hope in the things I wanted from Him. I found myself secretly basing my assessment of God's goodness on His provision of good things.

I realized that during much of my journey in praying for Charlotte, I had hoped so deeply for her salvation that salvation itself had become the thing in which I had placed my faith.

Even our desire for the salvation of our loved ones can become darkness within us when it becomes the thing in which we place our hope. I was hoping in what God could do for Charlotte rather than hoping in God as Charlotte's Savior.

But when we point our misdirected hope in miracles back to the Miracle Worker, the light returns.

Reflection Room

Request: Lord, please reveal to me the areas in my life where my hope rests in the good things You might do rather than in Your nature, Your character, and Your love. I have seen the evidence of Your goodness in Your Word and in Your faithfulness to me. I praise You for Your goodness. As in Luke 11:34–35, would You please give me healthy eyes that look to You as a proper source of hope?

A Heart of Flesh

As you've probably gathered, I've been blessed with many lost people in my life whose character could stand with that of the best Christians I've ever met, especially when it comes to specific acts of kindness, inclusivity, hospitality, and encouragement. The Lord has used these people to bless me and bring great joy and celebration into my life. I feel lucky to know them.

My friend Maria is one of the most empathetic listeners I know. She studied psychology in school, and few friends have ever so deeply met my need to be heard in moments of distress.

My mentor Sean was the first person to champion my career and promote me within our company. From him, I learned what humble confidence and gentle leadership look like.

My teacher Angela believed in me, even when I did not, and under her supervision and coaching, I excelled in my extracurricular activities in ways I didn't think possible.

Through my relationships with these lost friends and others, the Lord has given me many joyful moments. But every so often, I see glimpses of the wickedness of those who are far from God.

It shouldn't surprise me. I know the seriousness with which God considers sin, including my own. I know the creation story, and I'm familiar with the passage in Genesis where the Lord observes the evil of man. Genesis 6:5 reveals, "The LORD saw how great the wickedness of the human race had become on the earth, and that every inclination of the thoughts of the human heart was only evil all the time" (NIV). This verse sticks with me as I examine my own sin-inclined heart.

Knowing that even my own heart—one in the continual process of sanctification—is evil, I shouldn't be caught off guard by the evil in people who are far from God. And yet, I sometimes am because I see the Lord's design in these men and women. I see that He formed them—mind, body, and spirit. I know He endowed them with gifts, strengths, and qualities in His image to bring Himself glory and to point back to His kingdom.

I don't view myself as better or superior to these friends in any way. I certainly don't claim to behave perfectly, or even well, all the time. But I recognize some key differences in how sin impacts my life versus how it impacts the lives of the unsaved people I love.

As Christians:

- We recognize that our sins have been paid for, covered by a Savior.
- We have the great privilege of the Spirit's indwelling to correct and convict us.
- We are (hopefully) obeying the Lord's command to repent and ask for forgiveness.

- We have a Lord to whom we are being conformed, and our lives (hopefully) display the Lord's working and His grace as we spiritually mature.
- We are ever on the journey of becoming extensions of Christ to a hurting world.
- We are fighting against the sin in our lives by way of the power of God. We certainly couldn't do it on our own. No one can.

With Christ, we have been redeemed from our sins, and we've been given new hearts. We are being conformed to Christ. But what of our loved ones who have not yet begun to be conformed to Christ?

In Ezekiel 11, the Lord speaks to Ezekiel regarding those whom He will bring back from exile to the nation of Israel. There was once much idolatry and wickedness in the land, but He declares that upon the return of the Israelites who have been scattered across the nations, the idols will be removed. The Lord says, "I will give them an undivided heart and put a new spirit in them; I will remove from them their heart of stone and give them a heart of flesh" (v. 19 NIV).

Later, in Ezekiel 36, speaking of the restoration of Israel and the return of the exiles, the Lord says, for the praise of His glory:

> For I will take you out of the nations; I will gather you from all the countries and bring you back into your own land. I will sprinkle clean water on you, and you will be clean; I will cleanse you from all your impurities and from all your idols. I will give

you a new heart and put a new spirit in you; I will
remove from you your heart of stone and give you a
heart of flesh. And I will put my Spirit in you and
move you to follow my decrees and be careful to
keep my laws. Then you will live in the land I gave
your ancestors; you will be my people, and I will be
your God. (vv. 24–28 NIV)

In conforming His people to Himself, the Lord repeatedly empha-
sizes the gift of a new heart—one that is softened to Him and inclined
toward obedience, which leads to abundance.

Our unsaved loved ones have hearts that are inclined toward the
world. In much the same way that the Israelites of Ezekiel's time worshipped idols of their creation, our lost loved ones worship themselves
and their own created idols. This is why the things they say, do, and
think sometimes catch us by surprise. We are building our lives on
different foundations.

When a person's heart is hardened to God and oriented toward
the world, that person's behavior conforms to the world's ways as
well. When we examine our politics, our systems by which we acquire
wealth, and our entertainment industry—to name a few things—it's
easy to see more than a handful of ways in which evil has penetrated
our fallen world. Evil has poisoned virtually every institution and
organization and even the foundations upon which they were built.
We're all part of this problem.

In the lives of my lost loved ones, I see worldly reasoning being
carried out as well. I see the wickedness of people who are far from
God. I confess that each time I'm struck with the observation, I find

it extraordinarily difficult to comprehend how these hearts will ever begin to be softened and turned toward God. And I confess that in this way, although it's unintentional, I doubt.

In these moments, I'm brought back to the questions I mentioned at the outset of this chapter. And I'm reminded that the root of doubt is unbelief. But in light of my knowledge of the power of God, which He has demonstrated time and time again, I identify most strongly with the father we're told about in Mark 9.

In this passage, Jesus is approached by a man whose son is possessed by an impure spirit. The father of the boy comes to Jesus, we're told, because the disciples were not able to drive out the spirit themselves. No doubt exasperated and scared, the father says to Jesus, "If you can do anything, have compassion on us and help us" (v. 22b).

Jesus, upon hearing this, replies, "'If you can'! All things are possible for one who believes" (v. 23).

Upon recognizing the doubt in his heart, the boy's father immediately cries out in repentance, "I believe; help my unbelief!" (v. 24).

Reflection Room

Recall: Matthew 19:16–26. After Jesus speaks to a rich young man about eternal life, His disciples pose a question: "Who then can be saved?" (v. 25b). Then "Jesus looked at them and said, 'With man this is impossible, but with God all things are possible'" (v. 26). Our doubting may come from our inability to understand how salvation is possible for our loved ones. We're reminded here in Scripture that without God, it wouldn't be possible. Our reasoning on its own can never produce hope.

Help My Unbelief

When I'm tempted to rely on my human reasoning to work out the salvation of my friends, I fail every time. Much like the father of the boy in Mark 9, I've been waiting for change for a long time. We're told the boy has been demon-possessed since childhood, so it's safe to assume this man has been waiting quite a few years. He comes to Jesus, wanting to believe things can change, but he's desperate. He's running out of hope. He scrounges up what little faith he has left to ask Jesus if anything can be done.

I understand. That's where I so often find myself as well—on my knees before God, crying out for help in what feels like a hopeless situation. And in those moments, I'm reminded of the goodness and sovereignty of God. I'm prompted to repent of my doubt and cry out to the Lord, "Help me overcome my unbelief!"

The Lord has reminded us in the book of Ezekiel and in many other places in His Word that, despite what looks to us like long odds, He has the ability to change hearts. He can turn evil idolatry into righteous worship. He, for the sake of His glory, can do all things.

If God can save even us, then He can reach the people we love.

In a deep conversation with my wonderfully empathetic friend Maria, I asked about her thoughts on how a person begins to change their viewpoints when they don't want to change, when they don't know the consequences of remaining the same, and when they aren't even remotely aware that they need to change. Maria responded that, considering all three qualifications, it sounded like our hypothetical person probably *couldn't* change because they were not yet *willing* to change. And in many ways, she's correct, especially as it relates to faith.

The Lord knows the hearts of all our friends. He's not a passive God. He's intimately involved in the details of our lives, and He is pursuing the people we love. It is His great desire, even more than it is ours, that our friends and family would one day know Him as their Father. He's not the kind of Father who walks away either. As He works within and around them, He knows when they are ready to be given new hearts. He does not delay. And He doesn't rely on our observations either. He sees all the things we can't. He is not, as Peter reminds us in his second letter, moving in slow motion, though it may feel like it to us:

> But do not overlook this one fact, beloved, that with the Lord one day is as a thousand years, and a thousand years as one day. The Lord is not slow to fulfill his promise as some count slowness, but is patient toward you, not wishing that any should perish, but that all should reach repentance. (3:8–9)

When your heart is discouraged over the wickedness in the world, remember that our own hearts are also wicked. Genesis 6:5 does not allow for exceptions. Yet God still pursued and called us to Him. If God can save even us, then He can reach the people we love. He is transforming hearts and minds in His timing. We are all sinners for whom Christ gave His life.

Prayer Starter

Lord, thank You for being reliable, consistent, trustworthy, and good, even when I cannot understand what You are doing or why. Thank You for Your ability to soften hearts in seemingly impossible circumstances. Thank You that through You all things are possible. Father, my heart breaks for my friends. Please be with me in my discouragement. Help me trust Your timing and detailed plans. Let my hope rest in You and Your sovereignty rather than in the things I want You to give me. Grow in me deep and unbridled trust. Help me overcome my unbelief!

Chapter 4

My Loved Ones Should See Christ in My Acts of Service

"I'm just so amazed by His goodness in that season."

The words of my friend Hannah piqued the interest of all the ladies I hosted for taco night. Just a year earlier, I'd sat in that same spot with Hannah as she cried very different words through inconsolable tears. A yearlong romantic relationship had met with an unexpected end. She'd thought they were headed for marriage. It was devastating.

I'd comforted her, spoken truth to her, cleared my schedule to be with her. I remember vividly her sincere appreciation. "I don't know what I'd do without you," she'd said. We walked that road of healing together for quite a few months.

All the ladies at taco night had the same question: "How did you get through that?"

I ... may have had some expectations for Hannah's answer. I could already hear her reply, "Without June, I wouldn't have made it through that season. She was so kind and so present. She spoke truth to me and comforted me."

But instead she said, "God just showed up for me. I can't even explain it. He's just so, so good. I was hurting, and I felt completely alone. He drew near to me in my isolation, and I've never had such peace. I knew I could heal."

What? Was I making this up? Was I even there? Did she remember me at all? It took me a solid couple of minutes to get over myself.

I love showing up in the lives of my friends. My love language leans so heavily toward acts of service that I often wish I were better at some of the other ones! I want the people around me to see Christ and experience His love through me. I keep my car keys at the ready.

After taco night, I spent some time reflecting on who was most glorified by the work of my hands. I was momentarily distracted by the omission of my name in Hannah's story, but then I realized how glorious and humbling it was that my friend Hannah felt the Lord's comfort in her hurting. Had I been involved in *that*? How much greater for someone to experience God's love through me than to experience mine alone. Hannah didn't need my comfort. I was powerless to comfort her hurting heart in that bleak place. But God's comfort—through me, through Scripture, through all her other sweet friends and family, and through her own relationship with Him—gave her peace in her pain.

It wasn't about me at all. It was about God's goodness, just like she said. Her story became even more surreal to me when I realized that God is powerfully working through all of us as we offer Him our time and talents. He's revealing Himself in ways we can't even imagine, and He's showing up *for* us and *through* us. I'd bet we all want to be conduits of His love.

There are so many ways we can serve the people around us with our time and talents. In fact, we're called to. As we're conformed to Christ, it's natural that we would desire to show up in a hurting world. Matthew 5:14 affirms, "You are the light of the world. A city set on a hill cannot be hidden." We are not told to hide or to isolate. In fact, Jesus even tells us the second greatest commandment is this: "You shall love your neighbor as yourself" (Matt. 22:39b).

And what's more, we're told to serve without an ulterior motive of reciprocity. Particularly in Luke 6 and 14, we're given directives to serve and give to those who either cannot or will not give back. We're called to display selflessness without expectations.

In answering this call, we can be eager to serve and quick to extend mercy. We can allow God to use challenging relationships to grow us more into the likeness of Christ.

But we may wonder why the world doesn't always see Christ in the way we love our neighbors. Are we failing to love well enough? Serve often enough? We may fall into false beliefs that if we could just try a little harder, give a little more, pray a little longer ... then they would surely see Christ in us. Sound familiar?

This can become a slippery slope, even leading us to accept mistreatment and toxic behavioral patterns, remaining loyal to our loved ones at the expense of our own well-being. It's possible to serve unwisely.

You probably know what I mean.

If you're anything like me, you love those tangible opportunities to show up in the lives of your loved ones. You've served often. You've prepared meals. You've publicly testified to your faith. You've followed

Christ's example of servanthood (Matt. 20:26–28). You've used your gifts to become His hands and feet in the world, "as good stewards of God's varied grace" (1 Pet. 4:10b). You've even tried to carry a selfless heart.

But, like me, you may have done some of this expecting your loved ones to see Christ in your goodness and to respond accordingly. Perhaps you're even seeking some recognition for your efforts. Or you may be serving beyond your capacity, sure that God will use your effort in the ways you've imagined and planned.

Unfortunately, wronghearted service can cause more harm than good. Our friends' salvation does not depend on our good works or good behavior. In attempting to achieve salvation *for* them by serving them well, we may have misplaced motives and be serving man rather than God. We may be focusing on *earning* our loved ones' salvation rather than accepting that it's freely given by grace through *their faith* in Christ alone (Eph. 2:8).

In serving the unsaved people we love, we would do well to remember that we are ultimately in service to the Lord. He has our primary allegiance. Our service to our neighbors flows from our submission to and relationship with God as we first and foremost seek Him.

If our acts of service are calculated, performed in the name of God to accomplish the ends we desire, we have missed the point. But we might not even be aware of our motives. Of all the people who lie to me, I do it best.

If we pray for the Lord to search our hearts and motivations and shine His light in the dark places, He will absolutely show up. It's a daily request I place before Him. The Lord doesn't need us to accomplish His purposes for Him or apart from Him. Rather, He invites us to come alongside Him as the Spirit conforms us to Christ.

Reflection Room

Wrestle: Are there acts of service in your life that are, if you're honest, a bit more calculated than altruistic? Are there ways you're showing up in the lives of your loved ones where you may need to resubmit your motives and expectations to the Lord? Consider asking Him in prayer to show you if this might be the case.

Release the Burden

When Charlotte lost a close family member during the pandemic, my heart broke with hers. She needed to travel to be with family for an extended time, so someone had to check in on her elderly cat quite frequently.

The only catch? Logistics.

Charlotte lives on a quiet, quaint city street lined with cherry blossoms and touched by the distant sounds of neighboring highways. Let's just say she's a bit off the beaten path. As the pandemic continued to change life in our city, our public transit options became unpredictable at best. Staff shortages and mechanical issues also contributed to the challenge. So getting from where I live to her apartment wasn't the easiest commute.

But for several weeks, nearly every day, I made the trek across the city. I found productive ways to spend the travel time—listening to audiobooks and returning messages—but it was nothing short of sacrifice. I canceled plans, woke up earlier, and organized my days around showing up and serving her well in her absence.

Even after she returned home, the public transportation challenge impacted us in more ways than one. Charlotte doesn't have a car, but once a month she volunteers at a food bank just outside the city. Rideshare prices soared, and the inconsistency of public transit that far outside the city limits made the commute needlessly long, so I offered to drive her. Sometimes, I'd join her in serving, and other times, I'd grab my favorite cup of coffee and wait with a good book before driving home together. I enjoyed our rides and conversations, and it saved Charlotte hours of time and hundreds of dollars.

And then there were all the little things. Refilling both of our water bottles during the trek to the break room. Leaving an encouraging sticky note on her desk during a hard day.

There were many ways I served Charlotte well. And she loved and served me in wonderful ways too. She checked in on me with care and consistency. She offered to pick up lunch when I was trapped on never-ending conference calls. She returned my encouraging notes.

Serving people doesn't have to be complicated or expensive. Sometimes it looks like just a few words on a sticky note.

Perhaps you are like me, showing up in the lives of your friends and family to put your love into action. But after months and years of what to me seemed to be sacrificial love and service to my friend, I wondered why God hadn't used my efforts more meaningfully.

I loved my friend as myself and begged God to let her see Him through me. In this case, my expectations weren't about what Charlotte would do. They were about how God would use what *I* was doing.

On the one hand, I desired to be obedient to God, but on the other, I wanted to see kingdom benefit from it. By God's grace, I eventually realized my misguided expectations. And even more, I realized that serving others garnered joy in and of itself. What God chose to do with my obedience was up to Him, not me. I got to show up and love my friend. He got to do the rest.

No act or speech or gift that we give is capable in and of itself of drawing our loved ones to Christ.

I wonder, though, if you might be like me in serving, giving, and sacrificing for lost loved ones while also maybe expecting—hoping—to see clearly the ways God is using it for His kingdom. Maybe you're desperately desiring that God will use you to reach the people you love in a way that only He can. You're wondering if He will.

This wondering isn't wrong, but the personal orchestrating is unproductive. No act or speech or gift that we give is capable in and of itself of drawing our loved ones to Christ. Certainly, when we serve our lost friends and maintain an active, loving presence in their lives, we become an extension of the life of Christ. These things are pleasing to God. But for all our good intentions, we are powerless to achieve someone else's salvation.

Taking on that responsibility will always leave us feeling overwhelmed and disappointed. I say that not to discourage but to give freedom. Learn from me, and release yourself from carrying that burden. *The weight of other people's salvation does not rest on your shoulders.* Give the Lord your burdens instead, for He cares greatly for you.

Reflection Room

Recall: Ephesians 2:8–9: "For by grace you have been saved through faith. And this is not your own doing; it is the gift of God, not a result of works, so that no one may boast," and Titus 3:5: "He saved us, not because of works done by us in righteousness, but according to his own mercy, by the washing of regeneration and renewal of the Holy Spirit." What do we learn in these verses regarding any works done by man as they relate to the gift of salvation?

Boast in Weakness

One isolated pandemic day, I walked alone for about an hour to a part of my neighborhood that overlooks the larger cityscape. It was dark and rainy, and there weren't many folks around. I wasn't in high spirits and didn't care for music or audiobooks that evening, so instead I talked to God about my frustrations and worries. I made it to my destination, and I looked out at the city. Its vastness was not lost in the winds or rain. As I took in the view, I prayed for the hundreds of thousands of people who call this city home, many of whom are far from God. Some even hate Him. The all-too-familiar burden of their salvation crept in.

There are just so many of them.

I felt very small and incapable. The mission felt impossible. I saw a desert of need in comparison to the tiny, almost imperceptible, water droplet of service that I might, on my very best day, be able to provide in my own strength.

Overwhelmed, I failed to acknowledge that the ability of man or woman is so, so small compared to God's sovereignty. I lost sight of the fact that the King of the universe would make up the difference between the greatness of the need and the weakness of me.

At the moment we come to the end of our abilities and arrive at our weakness, we also come to the beginning of God's greatness and strength. It's only here that we begin to understand: If we could do it all alone, then why on earth would we need God? It puts 2 Corinthians 12:9 into perspective: "But he said to me, 'My grace is sufficient for you, for my power is made perfect in weakness.' Therefore I will boast all the more gladly of my weaknesses, so that the power of Christ may rest upon me."

This doesn't make sense to a world focused on our own individual abilities. As believers, we can boast in our weakness because we have a God who makes up the difference—and what a vast difference it is. The end of us is the beginning of God. The end of our ability to save our friends and family is the beginning of God's great display of mercy exhibited in His pursuit of them.

This is good for our friends and family as well. If they could trust in us to save them, they wouldn't have a need for God either. They would also probably need to be quite afraid—I'm sure I would make for a very poor god.

It's in God and God alone that our loved ones are saved. Our weakness is a great stage on which God can present His greatest displays of strength and His finest mercies. And what's more—not only does God bridge the infinite gap, but He also tells us He will. So instead of worrying, we're able to rest. He tells us He will provide, and then He shows up every single time in His perfect timing. Not only does God *not* make us carry the burden, but He also doesn't want us sitting around worrying about it. How great is His care and love for us that He has planned to cover even our fears with His assurance.

> *At the moment we come to the end of our abilities and arrive at our weakness we also come to the beginning of God's greatness and strength.*

Acts 4:11–12 is often quoted in reference to the claims of other religions, forms of spirituality, or beliefs about the afterlife. It says, "Jesus is 'the stone you builders rejected, which has become the cornerstone.' Salvation is found in no one else, for there is no other name under heaven given to mankind by which we must be saved" (NIV).

If you've read and reflected on these verses, you've probably noted the obvious truth: Jesus is the way to salvation. *His* is the name by which we must be saved. But I realized my actions and effort sometimes didn't reconcile with what these verses declare. As I strove to serve my unsaved friends and family, occasionally serving or sacrificing in my own strength and not at the prompting of the Spirit, I realized I was putting some weight behind *my own name* as well. Some of my hope still rested with me rather than with God alone. I was trusting in *my* name.

We might be tempted to look at this passage and think it's referring only to other gods, religions, and belief systems. It's paramount to realize that it also applies to us. Our names are not the names by which our friends will be saved. So when we show up, serve, and volunteer our time, money, attention, or effort, we can do it to the glory of God, knowing that He alone saves. The responsibility is not on our shoulders.

There's another passage I've often applied to my career or to work I didn't want to do, and that's Colossians 3:23–24: "Whatever you do, work heartily, as for the Lord and not for men, knowing that from the Lord you will receive the inheritance as your reward. You are serving the Lord Christ."

I've recalled these verses on several occasions at work to keep me on track for tasks I've found challenging. But they can even apply to our ministries. When we realize that all our work, even that of a religious nature, is for and in service to God and not for man alone, it takes the weight of responsibility off our shoulders. We don't need to do the saving. We can show up and serve a God who saves and let Him handle the rest. Our service, even on mission, is for God and His glory. He alone will choose how, when, and if to use what we set before Him. In this way, we have freedom.

Reflection Room

Request: Father, please help me humbly submit my service to You. I know that I am weak, but I delight in You and rest in Your strength. Help me show up well in the lives of my loved ones, trusting that You will use the work of my hands in ways I might not immediately or ever understand. Guide me as I lean into Ephesians 6:7, "rendering service with a good will as to the Lord and not to man."

Freedom from Striving

One evening, I found myself discussing the ideas of effort and striving with my friend Lindy. We work out together and often grab a quick bite to eat afterward. Lindy grew up in a different religion than I did, but she walked away from her belief system in college. She climbed the corporate ladder quickly, and her work was everything to her. She taught me a lot about business, and she had some incredible stories. I enjoyed our dinners together. That night, we dined on the waterfront, so naturally we engaged in a multi-hour conversation about moral philosophy.

We spoke at a high level about a few secular ethics systems. Utilitarianism, for example, asks how one can achieve the most good for the most people. This philosophy is of particular interest to a few of my friends, including Lindy. Her actions, to the best of her calculated ability, seek to rightly serve as many people as possible.

I asked her what utilitarianism does with the guilt and shame that result from human error. As in, what if you mess up? Are there allowances made for mistakes, for the benefit of hindsight, or for trying harder to be "good" in the future? And what about the differing opinions on what is best for the most people across the spectrum of human judgment? What happens when you're accused of falling short of some perfect standard of performance? How do you bridge the gap between what you should do and what you actually do? And even if you are "good," how can you be sure it's ever *really* enough?

Lindy acknowledged the system's limits. She also struggled with these questions. In all our lighthearted dinner musings on the ideas of moral ethics, one thing was clear: individual redemption is tricky. It seemed to me that in many systems of secular ethics, the individual is regarded only as a part of a larger whole and not necessarily of any worth or value in his or her own right, especially beyond an ability to achieve a standard of goodness or to contribute to the larger body of humanity in measurable ways.

I am most definitely not a well-studied moral ethicist, though I'm learning more over time. In my conversations with Lindy about the idea of morality, we kept coming back to the same question and the same underlying confusion: In challenging situations, big and small, what is the relationship between the end and the means?

For example, some branches of utilitarianism might say that the ends of doing the most good for the most people justify cruel (or even just "slightly bad") means. Practically speaking, morality is determined by what promotes the most good. At the extremes, this is a tall order. While utilitarianism might align with Christianity in supporting something like women's suffrage, it would differ fundamentally in other ways.

The study of moral ethics systems could consume an academic lifetime, but here's one extreme example for demonstration. Let's say we had two patients in the hospital, one needing a new heart and one needing a new liver. Utilitarianism suggests that it would be acceptable to sacrifice one healthy person, since the organs of the *one* would save the lives of the *two*. One life is taken, but two are saved. The ends justify the means. In this system, the responsibility to make the call lies with humans.

Christianity, of course, takes a different approach. What I shared with Lindy was this: In God's eyes, the end never justifies whatever means are necessary. And that is because God is the end. God holds the end in His hand. We're called to simply conduct our lives—the means we employ—in obedient, surrendered ways that honor and glorify Him, exemplifying His love to a hurting world. The means are our responsibility, and the ends are up to God.

What if, in our transplant example above, the medical procedure failed, and all three patients died? What if one of the two patients in need of an organ died and the result was equivalence in terms of goodness achieved versus the expended cost? What about the hardship created for the family of the healthy person who was lost so that two patients might be saved? I could ask a million questions.

This brings me to the questions I always ask when studying any other moral framework:

- What about shame?
- What if we mess up?
- What if we get it wrong?

- Or what if we don't get it wrong but someone gets hurt anyway?
- What if other people don't agree with how we live or with the decisions we make in our limited wisdom?

I'm exhausted just thinking about all of it.

Graciously, God's got all that covered too. Unlike in every other system, in the Christian faith, God has an answer for our mistakes, failures, shortcomings, and limitations. We get the divine privilege of living in the freedom of obedience and reaping the harvest of His mercy.

God fills the shame gap. God stands in the guilt void. God looks at His broken, hurting creation and sees us trying our best to serve Him with our lives. He sees our inabilities and our weaknesses, and He says, "This changes nothing. You are My creation. You are My child. And I love you deeply. I will never love you more or less than I love you right now. My love is perfect, complete, and merciful. My love for you stands in the gap through Christ's sacrifice."

Lindy and I discussed a few other moral ethics challenges that night. As in my example from earlier, a lot of the focus was on the end result. But the common denominator was the human effort undertaken to achieve whatever result or behavior was considered to be ideal. The common denominator was all the calculating, figuring, contemplating, struggling, and, ultimately, striving to achieve whatever standard of goodness was desirable to each system.

In each of those systems, the onus is on humans. The burden is completely carried by the doer. There is no escape, and there is no opportunity for redemption after failure.

That's bad news in light of this reminder in Ecclesiastes: "Indeed, there is no one on earth who is righteous, no one who does what is right and never sins" (7:20 NIV). A person seeking perfection is guaranteed to fail.

But in Christ, there is no fear of unredeemable failure. The Spirit works in the hearts of believers, spurring them on toward obedience and godliness. We desire to be like God because we love God and because He loves us. First John 3:1 says, "See what great love the Father has lavished on us, that we should be called children of God!" (NIV). Even where we fall short, this love bridges the gap between our behavior and perfection.

We are no longer enslaved to our sin or our shortcomings, nor must we carry fear of failure. "For all who are led by the Spirit of God are sons of God. For you did not receive the spirit of slavery to fall back into fear, but you have received the Spirit of adoption as sons, by whom we cry, 'Abba! Father!'" (Rom. 8:14–15).

Where Lindy is striving, Jesus provides rest. He covers her inadequacy with His love.

So how is all of this applicable to us? Simply put, we can take away the same lessons. Remember that the means fall to us. But God is sovereign over the end. The striving we're inclined to in our humanity, the burden that we carry—we can set it down at the feet of Jesus. He bridges the gap of our imperfections, and He tells us He loves us anyway.

Honoring God with our lives shouldn't result in striving. In fact, it should offer us ultimate freedom.

When we're tempted to hold the weight of our loved ones' salvation in our own hands, trying to somehow accomplish it through our efforts and abilities, we can instead recognize how what we believe is different from other worldly philosophies. We don't need to find ways of accomplishing the most good for the most people on our own. We don't need to strive for an impossible standard of "goodness." We don't need to be anyone's savior. We have one already! And He says, "Stop striving and know that I am God; I will be exalted among the nations, I will be exalted on the earth" (Ps. 46:10 NASB).

He tells us to follow and worship Him, to be sanctified in the means, and to trust Him with the end. In fact, He goes so far as to remind us of our limitations. He doesn't seek to belittle us or demean our worth but rather to implore us to rely on His strength instead of our human ability. In James 4:14, we're reminded, "Yet you do not know what tomorrow will bring. What is your life? For you are a mist that appears for a little time and then vanishes."

Who are any of us to think that we hold the power of life and death? Instead, God loves us enough to take away the pressure of our performance. He calls us to Himself so we can find rest, an invitation that stands in stark contrast to the weariness of a striving world.

Reflection Room

Wrestle: Do you carry shame for ways in which you feel you haven't done enough? How might your perspective change if you understood that the results of your service belonged to God alone?

Share in Wise Measure

There's one more thing we should talk about when it comes to service. Since you're a believer, your life can be an extension of the life of Christ in both your actions and your words.

Of course, there's a time and place for discussing matters of faith. Evangelism is of critical importance, but we are free to love people without injecting God into *every* conversation. Follow the prompting of the Holy Spirit and pray for the ability to discern when sharing is wise and fruitful.

That said, there's no need to shy away from faith-based answers when they're reflective of the truth. I'm a big proponent of not filtering out my faith for different audiences.

My friend Charlotte would occasionally wonder how I came to certain decisions. Often, the answers were prayer, fasting, or time in God's Word. I didn't shy away from sharing my process. I didn't do so in a way that was preachy or grand but rather as matter-of-factly as the matter, in fact, was. When faith is the foundation of our lives, it will come up naturally in conversation and will inform our reasoning and decision-making.

We will not convince someone of the truth by winning an argument—or by creating one at every opportunity.

But be released, friend, from the pressure to repeatedly present an exposition of the gospel. You in your human ability will not be able to convince anyone, especially if you're constantly interjecting at inappropriate moments or in insensitive ways.

A few of my close family members who don't believe in any god explored Christianity for a while, even reading one of my favorite books, *Mere Christianity* by C. S. Lewis. Lewis presents the best reasoning I've ever read about the existence of a higher power. And yet my family seemed to have rebuttals for all of it. Some of their answers to seemingly unexplainable historical events even made some degree of sense. But some didn't—at least not in my book.

The people we would love to convince of gospel truth will have their reasons for not believing, valid or not, logical or not. Our human efforts alone will not be strong enough to overcome these barriers. I have learned to let my loved ones tell me about their day, their work, and the other things that are on their minds without shifting every conversation to the topic of faith.

We will not convince someone of the truth by winning an argument—*or by creating one at every opportunity*. No amount of apologetics, biblical wisdom, or historical knowledge will convince a heart that hasn't been called to God by God Himself. Attempting to debate, reason, or explain *without ceasing* is an exercise in futility.

Maybe you have a relationship in your life in which you feel like your witness is the only gospel exposure the other person has. Perhaps you're a parent whose child is on a prodigal journey. My heart breaks with yours.

In the urban metro center where I live, I often find myself on the other side of this experience: in conversations with these young adult children. I hear about parents who, in their immense grief and concern, can barely speak to their son or daughter without, in the words of several of my prodigal young friends, "shoving faith down my throat."

Maybe you also feel this desperate desire to convince your loved ones to believe. I have, on more than one occasion, tried too hard to work my beliefs into conversations even with my friends. It's not that I thought in the moment that doing so would be wise. It's more like I didn't stop to think at all. *I felt like I had to dive deep.*

It can feel like there's no time to waste, especially if we rarely talk to someone. What if we get only a few minutes a week or even less? Here's the thing: God needs servants, not bulldozers. He can and will break down heart walls.

We shouldn't be discouraged from bearing witness to Christ with our words. Fear-based filtering is never a good strategy. But we should pray for wisdom to know when such discussion is fruitful and valuable. We are free to show up to serve, to love, to share in wise measure, and to submit salvation to God alone.

Reflection Room

Reframe: Instead of viewing each interaction with loved ones as a time to change their minds, show up joyfully, viewing time together as an opportunity to present God's love in whatever way He leads. Rather than approaching every conversation with an agenda, bring a curious and open mind. Might there potentially be more opportunities to love others well if we create a safe relationship space that is free from constant pressure and expectation?

People Aren't Projects

I go on walks with my neighbor Erin every few months. Somehow, the topic always turns to religion. Erin wishes she could believe. She worries over death and wonders about the afterlife. Inevitably, every time we walk, her faith questions invade our completely unrelated discussion. In this case, it's actually not me interjecting but her asking.

I've shared the gospel with Erin about a half dozen times in three years. Each time, Erin arrives to our walks with a curious heart, seeking to know more and to understand what, why, and in whom Christians believe. And each time, I share my perspectives, answer her questions as best I can, and submit to the Spirit in stewarding His message well. It has never once felt like wasted time. Nor have I orchestrated or planned these situations or conversations. And when Erin decides she's no longer interested in discussing religion, we move on to other topics.

We should remember that there is no need to manipulate every conversation. We can rid ourselves of the pressure of presenting the facts repeatedly, especially when they are not welcome or invited. It's okay to let the overflow of the love of God in your own life occasionally speak for itself. Perhaps this is what it means to let our speech be "seasoned with salt" (Col. 4:6). Our aim should not be to overwhelm people with Scripture or history or to nag for change, even when we have the best intentions. Instead, our aim is to love people out of obedience to God, putting our faith not in our acts of service or in our ability to convince but rather in the perfect character and timing of an almighty Father.

God is working in the hearts of your people. They may not see Christ in anything, including us, if they aren't yet ready to see Christ. Our own salvation is not earned through works; neither is faith gained by works. This frees us to love and commune with lost people without expectation. When we look back on our lives, we surely don't want our love for lost friends and family to be some manipulative ploy, no matter what we're trying to accomplish. We want love to overflow freely. We want to be patient, kind, humble, selfless, slow to anger.

*God is working in the
hearts of your people.*

People aren't our projects. They're our friends and family members. They're our neighbors. They're our coworkers. They're our coaches, doctors, mentors, teachers. They're unique, image-bearing children of the Most High God. The Lord will never ask us how many people we converted. He will instead look at how we freely loved and how we exhibited our obedience to Him.

We can just show up in the lives of our friends and family members—saved or not—delighting in sharing the love of God. No ulterior motives. No expectations. No agenda. No pressure. No recognition needed. We can serve out of obedience to God for His glory alone. Let's make that our goal.

Prayer Starter

Oh Father, thank You for freely giving us Your grace by faith alone. While my ability to impact any human life is small, thank You for Your vast and boundless power. When I reach my end, You have barely even begun. Please search me and my motives, and show me places in my heart where I need to release my burdens to You. Please give me opportunities to serve my loved ones well, because obedience brings me joy. Please teach me how to serve them in a spirit of freedom rather than out of fear that eternal consequences may rest on my shoulders. Please give me rest from my striving.

Chapter 5

This Pain Feels Too Deep

I love fireworks. I love gazing up at the night sky, taking in the colors and the shapes. I love the energy and excitement. It's delightful. Whimsical. Exhilarating. My city celebrates Independence Day with grand fireworks displays lasting upwards of twenty minutes. Plenty of time to enjoy the show and snap some photos. I look forward to it every year, and I plan the perfect viewing spot.

The fireworks are launched from the same site each year, creating a beautiful 360-degree show. But a few years ago, there was an unexpected change to the launch site. And wouldn't you know it, the wind was not cooperating.

As soon as the first firework exploded, my view became marred by thick, dark smoke. I missed the entire show. From my vantage point, I saw only darkness. The beauty of the fireworks was completely obscured.

On my journey to peace in my waiting, I realized that pain behaves this same way. I'd try to be present in my life, but sorrow clouded out joy. Simple pleasures and genuine laughter seemed to be shrouded by thick gloom. I couldn't experience them anymore. Life and its happier moments were obscured by the heavy smoke of sadness.

If you too feel the *weight* of this wait, you are in good company. Acute pain can stem from the awareness that those we love most are separated from God. The tears I have cried on behalf of Charlotte and many other loved ones are too many to bottle. As each tear falls from my cheeks, I picture myself swimming in the ocean they create. I hear the phrase "grace like rain" and instead feel that "tears like rain" is more apt. If you feel this way too, know that I see the depth of your sorrow, and you are not alone in it.

For me, great pain is associated with one observation in particular: many of my loved ones are especially elevated in this life. Charlotte holds a leadership role at her company, and she is well respected in her field. She's earned multiple postgraduate degrees and has been featured on several podcasts. She's talented in all her extracurricular endeavors.

Even though she works in an analytical field, she's quite creative and crafty, always working on an impressive project. She's extraordinarily well-read. She speaks three languages and has traveled the globe. She has a wide circle of friends and volunteers at a food bank. And as if that weren't enough, she's a classically trained musician. She plays piano *and* violin. She's even won her fair share of local composition competitions. She's also financially stable. And she's the kind of person who shows up for her friends. She's reliable.

By the highest worldly standards, Charlotte is extraordinary. One might wonder if these impressive feats come with a certain amount of arrogance, but Charlotte is quite humble. She even has a lovely sense of humor.

But here's the thing with Charlotte, and perhaps with your loved ones too: With each passing day, she is striving for more. She's pursuing the next accomplishment. She's studying for the next degree. She's working toward that next professional appearance. She's even working on advertising this success to the watching professional world, since, after all, her reputation is everything.

She accomplishes all she can in this life because, in her belief, nothing is eternal. All that she can get, she gets while she's here. She makes the most of this life, striving almost mercilessly as she pursues one goal after the next. She asks, "What else is there to do?" By all her accounts, she's living life to the fullest before it's over forever.

Don't get me wrong: she's got her fair share of struggles and losses. No one's life is easy. But at least on paper, she has great success and great victory in the eyes of the world.

I bet you and I are praying for quite a few people. Their lives and activities and priorities will all look a bit different. The thing that strikes me is not what they've *achieved* but instead what they're *seeking*.

This realization hit me hard one evening. Many of our loved ones seem to be seeking all the things that *would* matter if there were no God: knowledge, accomplishments, accolades, honors, reputation.

There is, of course, some wisdom in pursuing professional goals, working hard, continuously learning, and showing up intentionally in our careers and relationships. But the Creator calls us back to Himself when we start to lose sight of wise pursuits or when we begin to place our hope in things of little eternal value. We can pursue these things, but we can't allow these things to define us. We can't place hope in our ability to achieve as much as possible.

One evening, as I pondered such things with some degree of amazement, I wrote the following sentiment in my prayer journal: "How much greater it is to have glimpsed this life, understanding little, but also to have glimpsed the life beyond this, than to have seen and understood fully this life, only to have all earthly knowledge and accomplishment perish eternally."

Everything we collect here—our status, our accolades, and our knowledge—will one day turn to dust. One day *very* soon. And our lost friends are blissfully unaware, placing their identities in all the wrong things. The pain of this realization is deep and heavy. It's the pain of knowing that almost everything our loved ones prioritize amounts to *absolutely nothing.*

Now, I certainly know that work is ordained by the Lord. It can even be richly enjoyed. Our work, and even our success in work, honors our Father. There is nothing inherently wrong with possessions, success, honors, accolades, knowledge, or a great reputation. What wonderful gifts these things can be when they are bestowed upon us by God and when we are aware of our place as stewards. How richly these gifts can point back to and glorify God before a watching world. God even often uses the works produced by His lost children for the glory of His kingdom. I've brought my thanks and worship to the Lord on many occasions when He's answered my prayers through loved ones who don't believe.

But we run into problems when the things of the world, rather than the glory of God and the spread of the gospel, become our sole pursuit, the pinnacle of our life's work. I don't intend to discourage us from enjoying our lives or the things in them but simply to say that our ultimate focus should always be the Lord and His eternal kingdom. It's also the focus that garners the most peace.

Isaiah 26:3 affirms the reward of fixing our eyes on the King:

> You keep him in perfect peace
> whose mind is stayed on you,
> because he trusts in you.

Reflection Room

Request: Father, I confess that I worry because my loved ones might not feel like they need You amid their worldly success. But even where their success might be big, please remind me that You are bigger. Comfort me in the knowledge that You are sovereign over their time and talents and that You are able to use those things to accomplish Your purposes, to bring You glory, and to call these lost souls back to You in Your timing. I know You see my confusion and my pain. I love You, Lord.

How Long, Oh Lord?

As I revisit these thoughts on success, I'm reminded of the young man in Matthew 19:21 who is told by Jesus that if he wants to inherit eternal life, he should sell his possessions and give to the poor. Only after doing so could the young man follow Jesus.

We can glean a lot from this encounter about what things are of true importance. This man seems to have a fair amount of wealth and possessions. We are given the impression that he is a man who has much.

I picture a well-rounded and respected person who approaches Jesus with decent intentions. When Jesus tells him that in order to follow Him, the man will have to give to the poor all that he has, he leaves, discouraged. In his case, we're told specifically that his focus is his possessions.

This passage teaches us that focusing first and foremost on possessions, reputation, lifestyle, or anything else in this life, rather than on following Jesus, amounts to nothing. It is total loss. It is meaningless. So, while it isn't painful to see my friends accomplish wonderful things, it is painful to see them *prioritize* those things over eternity, as we see the young man in Matthew do with his wealth. He chooses to amass wealth in this life and reap condemnation later. It hardly seems worth it.

So, on the one hand, there's pain associated with the sheer knowledge of Charlotte's separation from God. And on the other hand, there is pain associated with the awareness that all her efforts are ultimately directed toward things that are not meaningful in and of themselves. Do any of your loved ones come to mind when we consider these ideas?

We want our friends and family to know our holy, living God, to enjoy Him, and to find their identities in Him rather than in their accomplishments. The wait seems endlessly painful. I've written in my prayer journal too many times to count, "How long, oh Lord? Please come quickly."

Reflection Room

Recall: Psalm 13. Reflect on what the psalmist does in the face of his pain and longing. What are some ways you might apply this passage to your life?

How long, O LORD? Will you forget me forever?
  How long will you hide your face from me?
How long must I take counsel in my soul
  and have sorrow in my heart all the day?
How long shall my enemy be exalted over me?

Consider and answer me, O LORD my God;
  light up my eyes, lest I sleep the sleep of death,
lest my enemy say, "I have prevailed over him,"
  lest my foes rejoice because I am shaken.

But I have trusted in your steadfast love;
  my heart shall rejoice in your salvation.
I will sing to the LORD,
  because he has dealt bountifully with me.

God as Our Guide

As you read these words, perhaps you're thinking I'm free of this pain. Maybe you're wondering whether my peace might be circumstantial.

But the past few years have been perhaps the deepest season of pain through which I've ever walked. Sorting through the lies of the Enemy, reconciling God's love with my observed reality, and battling hopelessness in my relationships with lost loved ones have been among my greatest emotional challenges.

I have certainly not summited this mountain, though I am farther up the trail than I was back then. This climb is hard. And it seems like it just keeps getting higher and higher. This life is a steady, continuous incline. We don't experience the summit here.

I've often asked, "What's the motivation to even keep climbing?" My feet hurt, and I am tired. The steep trail before me leaves me exhausted before I even open my eyes each morning.

In order to serve our friends in ways that don't destroy us, we need to be firmly rooted in Christ.

I often picture this pain as a deep, black forest where the path is rocky and unclear. The underbrush is thick and thorny. Sometimes the clouds roll over and more pain rains down. The only light penetrating the dense growth is the lightning from the storms overhead. This got me thinking, How do trailblazers and sojourners cut a trail through this kind of path? Might they have some kind of ... trail guide?

As Christians, we can set aside our fear of the forest. We have the ultimate Trail Guide. And an inerrant map in God's Word. A

accurate
flawless reliable

trustworthy light to shine in the darkness. A straight and narrow path that will not mislead.

It's so, so hard, though, to actually trust Him. I *say* I do. I certainly intend to. But do my thoughts, my worries, and my ruminations give credence to my expression of trust?

There is intense freedom and incomparable rest in acknowledging that we can't blaze the trail alone and urgently and desperately need the help of our Guide. Even once we realize that we are stumbling through the forest, how do we begin to *rely* upon our Guide? When it feels like we can't take even one more step, how do we address the depth of our pain? We are so deep in this wilderness.

When you consider the suffering that this great care for lost friends and family has brought to your life, you might wonder, as I did, *Is it possible to care too much? Am I crossing some kind of invisible "care boundary" that others have been smart enough to stay behind?*

I've come to the conclusion that it is not possible to care too much about the salvation of the people we love. It is, however, possible to let our deep care affect us in ways that are ultimately more hurtful than helpful. It is possible to take *too much* responsibility over circumstances that God alone shepherds.

As much as we love these dear people, it's important to remember the reality that our lives are built on different foundations. The unrepentant people we love have built lives on worldly pleasures and reputational success. Our world is built on the living God and His Word. Our world is built on the finished work of Jesus Christ on the cross.

In order to serve our friends in ways that don't destroy us, we need to be firmly rooted in Christ. Unchecked pain of any kind can wreak havoc on the soul, destroying the good fruits and good works that the Lord has prepared for us. So before exerting care over the salvation of our friends, we should take great care to nourish our souls with the truth.

Part of this truth is the reality of how much God loves each of us. We have no greater evidence for this than John 3:16: "For God so loved the world, that he gave his only Son, that whoever believes in him should not perish but have eternal life."

The Bible doesn't present clear-cut answers to all of life's most challenging and intricate questions. It gives us a great deal of direction about how we should conduct ourselves, but it's not a step-by-step manual. There is still some degree of uncertainty associated with decisions we must make or circumstances we find ourselves in.

But one thing we don't have to wonder about is His love for us. It exceeds even our most extravagant imagining. God loves us despite all the things we can't understand about our lives here. We first and foremost follow God as our guide by spending regular and consistent time in the inerrant trail map of His Word. We remember who we are, and we look to who He is. We recognize our limitations, and we dwell on His limitlessness.

Reflection Room

Wrestle: Do you find that your thoughts wander more readily to your pain than to God's comfort? Might there be ways you can retrain your mind to dwell more on unseen beauty than on seen sorrow? Consider adding a brief, consistent prayer time to a new part of your day or creating a prayer journaling routine. It's okay to start small.

His Love Is Greater

Armed with the knowledge of God's deep love and mighty sovereignty, I was finally able to look at my sorrow over my lost friends and realize that I was riding my care very nearly to the point of my destruction. I also realized that this wasn't helping anyone—not Charlotte and certainly not me. God didn't need me to take on pain that I was never intended to carry up the path.

So the first step in battling our pain is growing in the knowledge of His love for us. Our love relationship with the Father is the very foundation of our love and care for others. To care appropriately and without debilitating sorrow, we need to nurture our own hearts. We're told in Proverbs 4:23, "Keep your heart with all vigilance, for from it flow the springs of life."

I let my cares weigh me down, and that slowed me down. They drained my energy and distracted my focus. Can you relate?

The vastness and depth of God's love for us also puts our pain into perspective. As deep and wide as our pain is, the Lord's love for us is immeasurably greater. It might seem foreign now, but when we learn to focus on God by pursuing Him, our concerns for things in the world will fall in line, shrinking in comparison to God's greatness.

*When your suffering leads to
pursuit of the Lord, your care
is used for your sanctification
rather than your destruction.
You can operate from
peace rather than pain.*

But maybe you don't want your care to retreat or lessen. I understand. Rest assured that you will still care fully and deeply but in ways that foster trust in God and hope for the future, rather than in ways that lead to despair, destruction, and distraction. You are so much better able to care appropriately for and love your lost people when you're operating from the understanding of how deeply you are loved by God. When your suffering leads to pursuit of the Lord, your care is used for your sanctification rather than your destruction. You can operate from peace rather than pain.

Admittedly, this is easier said than done. Relationships don't happen overnight—even with God. They require consistency and engagement. Relationships need nurturing and *expressed* affection. They require intentionality.

As with the best relationships, experiencing intimacy with God is a continual journey. It didn't happen for me instantaneously but instead was pursued passage by passage, prayer by prayer, day after day, habitually. It's a relationship that I continue to pour into, investing time, attention, and affection. It is richly reciprocated.

Reflection Room

Request: Father, please give me strength to bring my pain to You rather than dwelling on it, burying it inside, or chasing after distractions. Use it to draw me close to You. I can't carry the weight of this sorrow, Lord, but I believe the truths of Psalm 145:8: "The LORD is gracious and merciful, slow to anger and abounding in steadfast love." Even as I love my friends and family, remind me of Your love for me. As with the psalmist in Psalm 18:16, please reach down and draw me out of deep waters. Thank You for being light in the darkness of my pain.

One Step at a Time

So what about the pain we're experiencing right now? We want to believe that God loves us and loves our friends and family, and we're growing in relationship with Him. We desperately desire peace. But sometimes it feels like it's hard to take even one more step. We might wonder if it's even worth it.

In one moment of deep pain, I remember wondering to myself, *Is this just the way I live now? Will sorrow always be hiding just below the surface, obscuring all joy and gladness?*

Shortly thereafter, one of my daily devotions focused on the name Emmanuel, which means "God with us." With that one word,

I remembered that we will exist in the presence of God for all eternity. Suddenly, I was struck with a suffocating despair. Eternity is a really, really, really long time. It's unimaginably and unfathomably long. And while I knew I would be spending eternity with God, I could find no peace in knowing that my loved ones might not be joining me there.

In moments like these, I would do anything for the Lord to rescue my lost friends so they could have my same inheritance. But then the Spirit gently whispers, reminding me to walk in the means and let God handle the end. By the grace of God, our position here also enables us to continue to intercede in prayer to a God who listens to and hears us. He loves our friends and family dearly.

We can't allow the pain to overtake us. After all, we're told that we will have tribulation in this life (John 16:33). And while our lives will have pain, that pain can be used for good.

This book, for example, is the product of deep pain. When I didn't know what to do with the overflow of suffering in my life, the Spirit prompted me to write. In this way, pain can be sobering and sanctifying, leading us to humble submission as we seek the Lord at our breaking points.

The problems occur when we don't submit our pain to the Lord. Without Him, our pain becomes hopelessness. This is the Enemy's chief goal. When affliction over the lost devolves into worry and hopelessness, we're distracted from our purpose in Christ. We're distracted from the fact that God is good. We're distracted from the all-important reality of God's deep love for us.

If affliction over the lost people in our lives is stealing our joy and distracting us from our relationship with God, then it's no longer righteous concern but has crossed the threshold into worry and perhaps even mistrust.

When pain begins to sow seeds of doubt in God in your heart, do not be dismayed or inclined to believe that there is no way out. We can turn this destructive thinking around by intentionally working against it and fighting for peace.

Sometimes I do this by reading Jesus's words in John 10:10, in which He reminds us that "the thief comes only to steal and kill and destroy."

The Enemy has used my deep season of pain to sow seeds of distrust in God's goodness. John 10:10 reminds me that the Enemy is the thief of joy and that he works actively toward my destruction every moment of every day. He desires nothing more than to pull us away from God, and all the better if he can do so through our own suspicion, doubt, and distrust. We're tricked into thinking that God, rather than the Enemy, is the one up to no good.

Do not let the Enemy distort your godly love for the lost and turn it into hopeless pain. This is not what the Lord desires for us. He wants us to find peace by intentionally placing our trust in Him. But that peace is not a state of being that we enter into permanently. Rather, it requires a daily pursuit of trust in God that doesn't give the Enemy space to steal it away.

Pain is an inevitable reality. We shouldn't run from it, and we can't make it go away. Sometimes, it demands to be felt. But the best way to deal with our pain, unmet expectations, disappointments, and confusion is to submit them to God. Trust won't happen by accident. It is boldly and intentionally pursued, despite how we feel. It is sought after and cherished.

My pastor wisely implored us in one of his messages, "Prayer and worship are not always a response to your emotions.... Sometimes prayer and worship are a revolt *against* your emotions."[1]

We can convert deep pain into deep praise. If we're able to wait well with a spirit of trust and hope, we can live victoriously despite brokenness.

Reflection Room

Recall: Encouragement from the Psalms. Consider committing the following verses to memory. Write them down. Carry them with you as tools with which to do battle against waves of pain:

- Psalm 18:28 NIV
  You, LORD, keep my lamp burning;
     my God turns my darkness into light.

- Psalm 31:21 NIV
  Praise be to the LORD,
     for he showed me the wonders of his love
     when I was in a city under siege.

- Psalm 34:18
  The LORD is near to the brokenhearted
     and saves the crushed in spirit.

This Glorious Sadness

I love animals. All kinds of animals. And also pictures of animals, especially kittens. I have a lot of plush animals too.

As much as people laugh at the parodies, those animal commercials with the sad songs really get to me. If you're familiar with those commercials, you've probably seen the one that features Sarah McLachlan and her song "Angel." Every time I see it, my imagination runs to all the creatures large and small who need rescue. There's a line in the song—a heart cry—in which she is brought to her knees by a "glorious sadness."[2] When it comes to the pain of knowing that the people I love are unrepentant, there are no greater words to describe the grief that encompasses my soul—*glorious sadness*. Have you felt it too?

We can see the juxtaposition here. On one hand, we feel sadness. But on the other hand, we marvel at God's glory. Sorrow in light of God's sovereignty. Agony under the promise of God's freedom. That glorious sadness does indeed bring me to my knees, but it does so before a holy Savior. A Savior who covers my pain, sanctifying me and guiding me toward hope.

In bringing me to my knees, my sadness also draws me to God, leading me to glorify Him. When the pain overtakes you and you're struggling to find the light, remember that the pain can pull you closer to the Father, who will never leave or forsake you. He won't leave the people you love either.

In these moments, I've found it helpful to recall the verses from Psalms we've just examined, like Psalm 18:28. I memorize them. I let them sink into my heart. I cry out to the Lord in worship with these words on my lips. He does indeed keep my lamp burning. I thank Him for their truth and ask that He would help me believe them. We can ask for this every single day.

When we have fellowship with Christ in His suffering, we are more able to have relationship with Him and can look more like Him to a hurting, dying world in need of His light.

It will do our soul great good to remember that the Lord does not waste pain. Charles Spurgeon writes, "The spade of agony digs deep trenches to hold the water of life."[3] When we walk through seasons of deep sorrow, let it be our aim to rejoice and worship, even through tears, knowing that great trial brings great refinement. As we are refined and sanctified to look more and more like Jesus, His light can shine all the more through us. When we have fellowship with Christ in His suffering, we are more able to have relationship with Him and can look more like Him to a hurting, dying world in need of His light.

So, despite the pain, keep going. One step at a time, hour by hour. Pour your pain into prayer. Trade in your sorrow for praise. Keep moving forward, fighting for hope day by day while pursuing the Lord with all your heart, all your soul, and all your mind.

Pain won't depart from us. It won't go away. It won't ever disappear in this life. In fact, I don't even want it to depart from me entirely.

I want care and concern to continue spurring me into intercession for these friends. I want pain to continue transforming me into Christ's likeness. I want to live with a heart inclined toward the lost. But this doesn't have to lead to a life of misery. We can learn to respond to pain in ways that reap joy and that incline our hearts toward abiding in God. We can learn to live in His peace.

I'd encourage you to commit Habakkuk 3:17–18 and Psalm 42:5 to memory. I recall these truths in times of deep distress, when words fail me and I am at the end of my ability to endure. Armed with these verses, I am able to tearfully cry out the following words (and sometimes *only* the following words):

> Though the fig tree does not bud
>   and there are no grapes on the vines,
> though the olive crop fails
>   and the fields produce no food,
> though there are no sheep in the pen
>   and no cattle in the stalls,
> yet I will rejoice in the LORD,
>   I will be joyful in God my Savior.
>   (Hab. 3:17–18 NIV)

> Why, my soul, are you downcast?
>   Why so disturbed within me?
> Put your hope in God,
>   for I will yet praise him,
>   my Savior and my God. (Ps. 42:5 NIV)

Prayer Starter

Lord, thank You for the depth of Your love for me and the people I love. Thank You for welcoming me into Your arms in my deepest moments of sorrow. Thank You that even though I don't understand what You're doing, You're using my pain for my maturity and my sanctification. I am being drawn more closely to You. Please comfort me, for I am hurting deeply. Let me, even in my lowest moments, place my pain at Your feet. Please do not waste this struggle, but refine me that my life might be used even more for Your glory. I rejoice in You, Father, and my hope is in You, even though I walk through this dark valley.

Chapter 6

I'm Disappointed in God

Ringo loves Q-tips. He has a lot of odd affinities, but he loves Q-tips the most. He collects them secretly. Hides them. Stores them up. He takes them places.

I should clarify—Ringo is my cat.

When I realized the extent of his love for Q-tips, I started to give him one every so often. Once he learned how to open the drawer, we had bigger problems. After I came up with a new storage solution, I regained control of the situation. Ringo still got his occasional Q-tip—but there were some left for me too.

I did notice one thing, though: I never saw as many Q-tips around my small condo as I'd given Ringo. *They must be under the bed or other furniture*, I thought.

Time got away from me once, and I realized I hadn't washed my duvet cover in a while. That sounded like a lot of effort, but it needed to happen. I unbuttoned the cover's side and untied the corners. As I removed the down comforter, hundreds of Q-tips poured out like a waterfall.

Ringo had been building his Q-tip kingdom.

By day and by night, in silence and secrecy, he had gathered his collection. He had been busy. He had been working. How long *had* it been since I'd washed the duvet cover? I didn't want to think about that part!

Kingdom building takes time. It's a labor of love. And it's something we may not often see. It's happening behind the scenes, outside our view.

If those Q-tips had been valuable or important to me, I'd have probably felt disappointed when they all went missing. I wouldn't have trusted Ringo to take care of them anymore. His Q-tip privileges would've been revoked. The only Q-tip kingdom builder I'd trust in that situation would be *me*.

When it came to eternal kingdom building, I realized I'd actually felt the same way. *Where are all my friends and family members? Why are they missing?* I couldn't quite pinpoint what I was feeling at first. It was a different kind of weight. It wasn't quite pain, and it wasn't unfairness. It was a deep disappointment—but not in my loved ones or in my own effort.

As hard as it may be to admit, we can feel disappointed in God.

A nagging, all-too-familiar question tugs at my mind's edges: *If God really is good, how can all these people still not know Him? Why haven't my loved ones been added to His growing kingdom?*

But I do trust God, and so I'm drawn to the logical question that follows: *Why do I think that the beliefs of my friends and family have anything to do with the Lord's goodness?*

This question brings us to one of the great paradoxes of faith, at least for me: the notion that circumstances are evidence of the goodness of a holy God. The idea that if God is good, He wouldn't let our friends or family members continue to walk apart from Him. This might lead us to ask: Even if God is good, *what good* is God? Or what good is following Him obediently without the people I love most alongside me?

These questions may seem extremely bold and overly direct. I felt a degree of discomfort just typing them. And yet, I'd bet that in moments of deep distress we've all wondered something like these hard questions. God certainly knows if we've struggled with such thoughts. The hard questions of faith are not the problem; the problem is what we do with them. If we let our unanswered questions sink us into the pit of despair and we take our complaints to the world—to our friends, to our addictions, to our distractions—then our hard questions kill our relationship with our Creator.

The hard questions of faith are not the problem; the problem is what we do with them.

But if we look in the face of our hard questions and we take them to God and His Word to search for answers (or even comfort), then our hard questions are not only welcome but beneficial. Our hard questions can draw us closer to our Father, who welcomes us—and our questions—with open arms.

God might be more faithful than we realize, even when circumstances feel more bad than good. In these moments, we can revisit the journey of the Israelites in Exodus. In their journey out of Egypt, the Israelites are weary. They feel worn down and are hesitant to trust God. But that doesn't stop God from showing up powerfully on their journey, time and time again. Right after the Israelites flee Egypt, we're told that, "By day the LORD went ahead of them in a pillar of cloud to guide them on their way and by night in a pillar of fire to give them light, so that they could travel by day or night" (Ex. 13:21 NIV).

That's some pretty powerful stuff. I've had some extraordinary interventions in my life at the hand of the living God, but I'd wager that if I'd been among the people on the journey in Exodus, I might have at least noticed that having a massive cloud pillar floating around was a bit ... peculiar. But only eleven verses later, in Exodus 14:10, the people realize they're being pursued by a mighty Egyptian army, and they're terrified. They begin to make assumptions about why they've been brought out to the desert: maybe to die! They doubt the Lord and are disappointed in His provision.

Shortly thereafter, in chapter 14, the Lord parts the Red Sea through His servant Moses. "The waters were divided, and the Israelites went through the sea on dry ground, with a wall of water on their right and on their left" (vv. 21b–22 NIV). And don't forget the pillar of cloud ... It's still there, dividing the Egyptians and the Israelites so the Israelites can pass through the sea unharmed.

Near the end of the night, we're told, "Then the LORD said to Moses, 'Stretch out your hand over the sea so that the waters may flow back over the Egyptians and their chariots and horsemen.' Moses stretched out his hand over the sea, and at daybreak the sea went back to its place. The Egyptians were fleeing toward it, and the LORD swept them into the sea" (vv. 26–27 NIV).

Neither the mysterious guiding pillars of cloud and fire nor the parted sea are enough to convince them of God's faithfulness. But at last we are told that after "the Israelites saw the mighty hand of the LORD displayed against the Egyptians, the people feared the LORD and put their trust in him and in Moses his servant" (Ex. 14:31 NIV).

There is praise and singing to the Lord for His greatness and power (Ex. 15:1–2). But how quickly the Israelites again become disappointed in His provision. As they travel away from the sea and through the desert, their hunger is tested, and they grumble against both Moses and the Lord, assuming that they will now come to ruin (16:1–3). The Lord, though, is faithful, quite literally providing their daily bread (v. 15).

Our hard questions can draw us closer to our Father, who welcomes us—and our questions—with open arms.

We're not all too different from the Israelites in the desert, are we? We forget the Lord's goodness when we're under pressure, when we're scared, and when we're deeply suffering—especially when the pain has continued for a long time. We might've started out with great faith, but the cumulative effect of waiting for change has worn us down. We are so tired. It sometimes doesn't feel like any small, good thing around us could come close to lessening the burden we feel.

We might even struggle to see God protecting us, providing for us in little ways, as we walk through the tedium of daily life. The sky isn't raining bread, we say. And the clouds ... well, they look pretty normal. I don't see any great cloud pillars leading me or my loved ones in any direction.

Yet He tells us He is faithful. We can look to Psalm 3:5: "I lay down and slept; I woke again, for the LORD sustained me."

By God's Word, we can remember: we are alive at all only because the very will of God continues to produce breath in our lungs. Exhale disappointment and breathe in His faithfulness.

Reflection Room

Wrestle: Even though you believe God is good, do you ever struggle to live into that reality? Do you experience disappointment in an area of His provision? Recall a few times in which God has displayed His faithfulness in your life. Consider writing them down. Ask Him to allow you to see Him at work around you and to draw your attention to His work, even in small places.

Keep Knocking and Keep Asking

Sometimes, our disappointment can become so heavy and our worries so intense that sorrow steals all joy. Disappointment is the cousin of hopelessness. We're weary, and we wonder, *How much longer?* We begin to sow seeds of doubt in gardens where God's goodness was growing. Disappointment opens a rift between us and God, and where we once abided in Him, we now abide in our unmet expectations.

When we feel empty or deflated, as though the wind used to fill our sails but now the breeze has died down, we can end up dwelling in that windless place, stranded on open seas. We feel alone. Rather than seeing our Father in heaven, we simply see what's right there, or rather, what's *not* right there, in front of us. *A lens of disappointment causes us to see what's missing instead of what's present.*

Within the realm of our human experience below heaven, we will no doubt walk through seasons of disappointment. Life in a broken world guarantees it. The kind of disappointment I'm talking about here, though, goes further than circumstantial sorrow. This is disappointment in God for the things we think He should be doing for us and especially for the people we love.

At the end of every day, I write a paragraph or two in my prayer journal, and I always close by asking God to save my sweet friends and family members. I'd estimate that I'd written Charlotte's name in my prayer journal a little more than three hundred times when I experienced a particular sense of disappointment one night.

It wasn't necessarily hopelessness. I still believed that Charlotte could be saved one day. But I felt my optimism deflating because God had not yet answered. *Is He ignoring me? Have I done something wrong, either with Charlotte or with Him? Should this delay cause me to question Him? Is it even worth it to keep asking?*

Have you ever felt this way in your waiting?

After asking these questions, I remembered the parable of the friend at midnight, in Luke 11:

Then Jesus said to them, "Suppose you have a friend, and you go to him at midnight and say, 'Friend, lend me three loaves of bread; a friend of mine on a journey has come to me, and I have no food to offer him.' And suppose the one inside answers, 'Don't bother me. The door is already locked, and my children and I are in bed. I can't get up and give you anything.' I tell you, even though he will not get up and give you the bread because of friendship, yet because of your shameless audacity he will surely get up and give you as much as you need.

So I say to you: Ask and it will be given to you; seek and you will find; knock and the door will be opened to you. For everyone who asks receives; the one who seeks finds; and to the one who knocks, the door will be opened." (vv. 5–10 NIV)

I laughed, imagining myself as the protagonist banging on God's door at three in the morning for days and weeks on end, requesting the same things for the same people. And I thought, with a grin, *See You again tomorrow, God.*

The story teaches us that we can shift our focus off our observed reality—our disappointment—and instead cast it on the Author of reality with a renewed vow to *just keep knocking.*

Even if our asking doesn't result in immediate change, no harm can come from us interceding with our heavenly Father on behalf of our friends and family. After all, we're told in Luke 11:11–13, "Which of you fathers, if your son asks for a fish, will give him a snake instead?

Or if he asks for an egg, will give him a scorpion? If you then, though you are evil, know how to give good gifts to your children, how much more will your Father in heaven give the Holy Spirit to those who ask him!" (NIV).

This doesn't mean we'll always get what we ask for. But it does communicate quite clearly that God gives good gifts to His children and that He does not desire to harm us. He doesn't desire us to walk in constant disappointment. So not only can we keep asking, but we can do so with the expectation of experiencing God's goodness in return. The Author of reality is writing a better story than we could ever write ourselves.

Reflection Room

Reframe: Instead of dwelling on ways God seems to be absent, practice viewing the void as a vast arena in which He is still working out the details of His love behind the scenes. Recognize and celebrate the obedience in your continued asking while still expecting to see His goodness, even in unexpected ways.

Read James 1:17. Recall a time when God demonstrated His goodness to you in an unexpected way: "Every good gift and every perfect gift is from above, coming down from the Father of lights, with whom there is no variation or shadow due to change."

Take Refuge in God

This brings us to the concept of refuge: the way in which we dwell in
God and His goodness rather than in the circumstances we experience
around us. Our doubt over God's goodness will grow and our disappointments will compound over time if we're focused on that windless
sea—that unchanging, seemingly impossible circumstance in which it
feels like God is silent. When the sun beats down and there is no wind
in our sails, when the sea is flat and motionless, God covers us with His
mercy while we wait.

If you were to do a quick search for Bible verses about refuge, what
you would find might surprise you. The occurrences are too numer-
ous to list here. Psalms is particularly rich in references to refuge. The
psalmists, while experiencing various types of pain, fear, discomfort,
isolation, and even doubt, repeatedly press into this idea.

Psalm 91, which in the ESV is titled "My Refuge and My Fortress,"
offers this depiction:

> He who dwells in the shelter of the Most High
>   will abide in the shadow of the Almighty.
> I will say to the LORD, "My refuge and my fortress,
>   my God, in whom I trust."
>
> For he will deliver you from the snare of the fowler
>   and from the deadly pestilence.
> He will cover you with his pinions,
>   and under his wings you will find refuge;
>   his faithfulness is a shield and buckler. (vv. 1–4)

A wise friend told me she often pictures this quite literally. In times of distress, she vividly imagines seeking physical refuge in our Father. In the NIV, verse 4 of the passage above reads,

> He will cover you with his feathers,
>   and under his wings you will find refuge;
>   his faithfulness will be your shield and rampart.

When we reach the end of us—when disappointment chokes out hope and we just need rest from our weariness—we can ask God boldly to shelter us under His wings. We can meditate on (or cry through) Psalm 91. We can beg God to meet us with His comfort and rest and to show us continually how to take refuge in Him as our protector.

One way to practice taking this refuge in our Father is to live out the advice in Philippians 4:6, "Do not be anxious about anything, but in everything by prayer and supplication with thanksgiving let your requests be made known to God."

When we're driving to the next errand and that familiar pang of sorrow for our lost family member hits us, we can take their name and our sadness to our Father. When we're staring into our open refrigerator and we're hit with that desire to share a meal with a friend for whose salvation we're waiting, we can lay our pain at God's feet and ask Him to show us how to rest in His goodness. When our minds wander in that work meeting and we can't shake the nagging thought that our coworkers might never be saved, we can ask God to be with us in that moment, to comfort us and to be the lifter of our heads.

We can also ask our Father to show us His merciful loving-kindness and to let us see and experience His goodness, even in small ways, as we wait.

We're told in the next verse in Philippians 4 that He will meet our requests with His mercy: "And the peace of God, which surpasses all understanding, will guard your hearts and your minds in Christ Jesus" (v. 7).

I find journaling particularly helpful to avoid falling into the short-term memory problems the Israelites had. When God provides for me, when He protects me, when I experience His provision, I note it in my prayer journal so I can be mindful and grateful for every blessing He brings to my life.

Sometimes, the refuge He provides comes in the form of a call from a friend. Sometimes it's a verse from the Spirit when I need comfort. Sometimes it's sleep that had previously evaded me. I write these things down, and when I page through my journal entries over the years, perhaps just when I'm beginning to think that God is and always has been silent, I see all the verses He's brought to my mind; all the friends He's supported me through, even in the smallest of ways; all the small, joyful moments that were evidence of His goodness to me, even in seasons of deep pain.

We can seek refuge in God simply by including Him in our lives. We can talk to Him, tell Him how we're feeling, tell Him what deeply troubles us—over and over and over. When I think about my deepest relationships, like the one I share with my mom, some feelings come to mind: safety, warmth, security, gentleness, and kindness ... to name a few. Sometimes, when I've needed to take refuge, I've sought out my mom. *Depth of relationship forges a path to refuge.*

As we invite God into our lives—as we start to acknowledge His hand in small details and to share our thoughts, feelings, and burdens—we grow a relationship of refuge for our daily lives, especially when we see nowhere else to turn.

My mom is a great problem solver. She gives good advice, she listens well, and she loves selflessly. And yet, even she doesn't hold my tomorrow. She doesn't orchestrate the details of my life, nor can she control even the smallest hair on my head. She loves me, most powerlessly. She is a beautiful gift. And yet there is even greater unmatched comfort to be found in taking refuge in our Father, who holds all our tomorrows, who holds the very souls of our friends and family in His hands, who in His mighty, merciful power is working all things for our eternal good.

We can seek refuge in our Father who loves us. We can even take to Him our disappointments—even if they're disappointments *in Him*. He will meet us with His love and comfort.

> Taste and see that the LORD is good;
>   blessed is the one who takes refuge in him.
>   (Ps. 34:8 NIV)

We're told in 2 Corinthians 10:5 to "take captive every thought to make it obedient to Christ" (NIV). There is no greater cure for unchecked disappointment and the emptiness that accompanies it than fighting through the hollow void by boldly declaring before God, "I do not understand what is happening, but I choose to believe that You are good and that You love me and the people I love in spite of what I'm able to see right now."

Fighting against disappointment is a choice, moment by moment, day by day, until it becomes a habit of surrender that enables us to abide not in our experiences in or expectations of the world but in the arms of the eternal King.

Reflection Room

Wrestle: What are some ways you might incorporate a practice of continual prayer into your life? Could you consider taking thoughts captive by going before the Lord in prayer, even briefly, each time disappointment strikes? A habit of prayer may reap a harvest of hope.

God Is Still Faithful

After so much talk on Exodus, I'd be remiss not to mention Exodus 14:14. Before the Israelites realize the Red Sea will be parted, the Egyptians will be defeated, and their lives will be spared, Moses tells them, "The LORD will fight for you; you need only to be still" (NIV).

The same holds true for us today. And He's not fighting for just us. He's fighting for our lost loved ones too. As we pray and intercede for them, the Lord is pursuing them in ways we cannot even imagine. Though we may feel disappointed by circumstances that seem unchanging, He's fighting for each and every one of us. He's building

His eternal kingdom, but unlike my cat, He's not filling it with Q-tips. He's filling it with His beloved children.

The best news isn't in the outcomes of circumstances around us, though—it's that we can take God at His word. When circumstances test our limits, we are comforted by the assurance that our pain will end: "For I consider that the sufferings of this present time are not worth comparing with the glory that is to be revealed to us" (Rom. 8:18).

God meets us in our brokenness, confusion, and disappointment, and He offers Himself to us.

We do see evidence of God's mercy in our lives, if only we are brave enough to find it. We can hope in this God who fights for us, even as we wait to see His mercy in hard places. Romans 8:24–25 reminds us, "For in this hope we were saved. Now hope that is seen is not hope. For who hopes for what he sees? But if we hope for what we do not see, we wait for it with patience."

Faith based on circumstances is rocky faith indeed. It makes idols of everything. It seeks help from everything *but* God. It looks at the things we deeply desire, and it says, "That is what I worship, so if I get it, I will have faith." But I've reckoned with a hard truth these past few years: if even a small amount of our faith is built on seeing the salvation of the lost people we love, we've made an idol out of their choices and their trajectory. No wonder this leads to disappointment.

Think back to Matthew 17:19–20, when the disciples were unable to heal a demon-possessed boy:

> Then the disciples came to Jesus privately and said, "Why could we not cast it out?" He said to them, "Because of your little faith. For truly, I say to you, if you have faith like a grain of mustard seed, you will say to this mountain, 'Move from here to there,' and it will move, and nothing will be impossible for you."

A small amount of faith is extremely powerful, even when it's misplaced. A small amount of misplaced faith—in things, circumstances, or results turning out the way we want—has the ability to wreck our lives, steal our peace, and destroy our trust. It robs us of the great wellspring of life: faith in a God who loves us.

When we make an idol out of salvation—when we worship it more than we worship God—it paves the way for disappointment in God, because we're basing our hope on the wrong thing. Our hope must be found in the Lord alone. We hope in Him because of who He is.

It's natural to hope for good things. To deeply desire God's providence and provision. To long for His good work in our lives. These things are right and pure when held in their proper place. But I had taken the things I wanted and placed them on a pedestal of holiness. Rather than worshipping God, I worshipped what I wanted from Him. In His mercy, God slowly revealed to me that rather than hoping *in Him*, I was hoping *in salvation*. I had made salvation my god, rather than trusting the God who gives salvation. I needed to learn how to hope *for* my friends' salvation but not hope *in* it.

Here's the good news: God meets us in our brokenness, confusion, and disappointment, and He offers Himself to us. After all, that's what salvation really is. That's what we want for our friends, and it's also what God wants for us. He wants us to know, intimately and personally, that He saw us, in all our brokenness, and He came in the flesh to meet us in our pain. Jesus came to meet us *where we are.*

We walk through hard circumstances. Bad things happen. We do not have all the answers. And often, we don't understand why. But He is there with us. He's the ultimate kingdom builder.

When God gives me His presence over His presents—when He shows up for me, when He comforts me, when He meets me where I am and tells me He sees me—I'm assured that I don't need any more signs or miracles in order to know that He is good. I'm no longer disappointed. I'm in awe.

> Oh give thanks to the LORD, for he is good;
>   for his steadfast love endures forever! (Ps. 118:29)

Prayer Starter

Father, thank You for being consistent and unchanging. You are good, even when things are not. Thank You for being the ultimate listener, welcoming my questions and my cries with gentleness and patience. When it feels like things aren't changing, please give me endurance to keep bringing to You my questions and my disappointments.

Please shower me in Your mercy, and teach me how to seek refuge in You. Convict me, oh Lord, when I take my disappointments elsewhere, and gently draw me back under Your wing. Teach me to rest in Your love as I continue waiting for Your answers to my prayers.

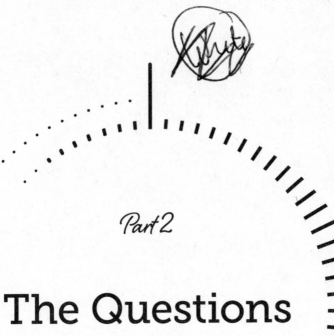

Part 2

The Questions
We Ask

Chapter 7

Does God Hear My Prayers for My Loved Ones?

I'd probably been talking for twenty minutes. My mom is such an incredible listener. My story had quite a few details to sort through. I backtracked a few times to recount important pieces I'd left out. It was a complex situation, and I wanted to hear her perspective. I needed her advice. Imagine my surprise when I finally asked for her thoughts and was met with only silence.

I asked again—"Hello? Did you hear any of that?"

More silence.

Had I just shared everything on my mind to an empty phone line? Would I have to repeat it all over again and try to remember all the details? That would take a lot of energy. *How disappointing*, I thought. I should've checked in somewhere at the ten-minute mark. What's the last thing she'd heard?

But finally, her voice came through the line: "Sorry! I accidentally hit my mute button. I heard everything you said."

What a relief. She had been listening.

It's discouraging to feel like you're voicing your story—your needs, your desires, your hopes—to an empty phone line.

Prayer felt that way to me for a while. Especially prayer for lost people.

Is there someone you pray for almost every day? Is there a voice you'd love to hear proclaim the name of Jesus? Maybe you're tired of bringing the same names to God over and over again, begging Him to move in a way that only He can. Do you ever wonder if He's hearing you—if He's on the other end of the line?

I understand. I pray for Charlotte every single day. Sometimes it's only for a few minutes—a few brief requests for her eyes to be opened, for her heart to be softened, and for her name to be written in the Book of Life. Other times, the need to pray at length for Charlotte and other loved ones comes on suddenly, accompanied by tears as I plead on my knees before the Lord.

In my daily prayers, I generally save intercession for last. And each time, it's accompanied by a certain heaviness. A thought that says, *Here we are again.* The excitement and expectation for salvation is sometimes overshadowed by the weight of another passing day. But I press on. I pray for them. I plead on their behalf.

Each time as I'm closing, I find myself feeling as though it's not enough. I'm not ready to leave each day's pleadings. *Just a few more minutes,* I think, *a couple more intercessions. Surely, there's something I can say, some way that I can word my desperation for their salvation that will cause God to move more swiftly so that I might not find myself here again tomorrow. What words have I left unsaid? I must need new synonyms or more eloquence.*

As with my acts of service, I've been tempted to think in my prayer life, *I'm doing my part. I'm praying unceasingly. So why doesn't the Lord open their eyes?* And one day, I felt a gentle nudge reminding me of the nature of Christ's sacrifice: *Salvation is relational rather than transactional.*

Allow me to explain. I did a brief stint in online dating. I downloaded a few apps, formed a panel of advisers from friends with online dating experience, and set out to explore this new frontier. I had some qualms and discomfort with the idea up front and received a lot of wise counsel and sound advice.

However, one friend on my panel of experienced daters counseled me not to consider outreach, like messages and likes, from potential suitors with much weighty emotion or apprehension. Online dating was merely transactional, she said. I was still developing a solid scriptural understanding of this part of life, but even then, something about the word *transactional* didn't sit well with me, especially in dealings with potential life partners.

I pondered this idea for a while and raised it with others. Much to my relief, I learned that no interaction with another human should be considered merely transactional. We all leave an imprint on one another's lives, whether positively or negatively, in sinful or God-honoring ways. Even such interactions as checking out at the grocery store or other encounters that genuinely seem like actual transactions can honor or dishonor Christ.

To put it pointedly, our biggest witness in our everyday lives isn't lofty or grand expressions or experiences of faith. It's how, by the fruit of the Spirit within us, we show up moment after moment in the lives of the people around us. When I hear the expression "Showing up is half the battle," I'm inclined to think, *And it's 100 percent of the stage on which we live out our faith.*

So if my relationship with strangers in an online forum shouldn't be viewed as merely transactional, how much more can we be assured the same holds true for our dealings with a holy God and His workings in the lives of His children? God's pursuit of His lost sheep is not a numbers game. Neither are our prayers. There is nothing transactional about it. God has a deeply personal, perfect plan for the lives of the people we love. Our prayers won't carve the path to all the things we want for them. Through our prayers, God is simply inviting us to be involved.

> Our earnest and steadfast prayers
> are critically important because they
> not only submit our requests to God
> but also incline our hearts to His.

We can submit our prayers to God and know that He hears us. I know this is easier said than done when it doesn't feel like God is listening, but in those moments, our feelings deceive us. He hears every word, including thoughts in our hearts that we may not have even directly spoken. Romans 8:26 says, "Likewise the Spirit helps us in our weakness. For we do not know what to pray for as we ought, but the Spirit himself intercedes for us with groanings too deep for words."

At the end of the day, when our feelings are heavy and we bow our heads in prayer, the Spirit intercedes for us where our words fall short. Our prayers do not lack any words needed for God to see into the depths of our hearts and hear our cries.

God not only hears our speech but also sees our intentions. We are deeply seen and heard. Carefully considered. We can let our requests be made known and then rest peacefully with the knowledge that the Great Orchestrator is working. The Maker is on the move.

Our earnest and steadfast prayers are critically important because they not only submit our requests to God but also incline our hearts to His. Faith, trust, and patience in the Lord's timing are much more easily experienced when constant prayer aligns our hearts with the Father's—and when we're praying for that alignment consistently.

Reflection Room

Request: Father, I deeply desire that You would open the eyes of my loved ones so that they would see their need for You. I'm so thankful that You know their hearts as well as You know mine. Thank You that Your dealings with them are not transactional but personal and patient. Even as I bring my repeated pleas to You, would You align my will to Yours? Let me rest in the knowledge that You hear my every prayer.

Pray without Ceasing

I'm tempted to focus so much on my own works and acts of service in pursuing my lost friends. I want them to see Christ in me. I want that to be enough. If we're not careful, we can overly focus on those acts of tangible service.

But be comforted in knowing that prayer is a great and mighty act of service on behalf of these people. All our service is good, but our prayers are perhaps the single greatest way we can love our friends and family. Charles Spurgeon writes, "There is profit in all labor, but most of all in the work of intercession."[1]

When it comes to our desires to serve our loved ones well, we should converse with them, share with them, serve them, and show up. But we should also use our energy wisely so it is not so focused on serving lost people that we neglect to intercede on their behalf in prayer. Prioritize going before the Lord in earnest prayer on their behalf over everything else. Trust that He hears you and is working in mighty ways, even when we can't see it through our limited perspective.

Prayer has powers of change beyond anything we could accomplish through the works of our hands. If we bear any responsibility regarding the salvation of our lost loved ones, it's that we use our time and speech according to the commands of God in 1 Thessalonians 5:16–18: "Rejoice always, pray without ceasing, give thanks in all circumstances; for this is the will of God in Christ Jesus for you."

We run into some complex and confusing circumstances in this life. We take them to the Word. We weigh them against its wisdom. We talk them through with wise counsel. But even then, we might not always know what we should do. That's a problem that particularly challenged me with people's salvation. I felt like I'd exhausted my resources. My heart hurt deeply, but I couldn't figure out what I should do about it.

I know how much our hearts ache over the lost people we love. When we let ourselves imagine an eternity without that parent, that friend, that child, it feels cruel and terrifying. It's almost too much to bear. These friends and family members break our hearts. These moments of intense sorrow are a small experience of our own Gethsemanes. One day, not knowing what I should do, I looked to see what Jesus did with His sorrow in the garden of Gethsemane, right before He was taken to be crucified:

> Then he said to them, "My soul is very sorrowful, even to death; remain here, and watch with me." And going a little farther he fell on his face and prayed, saying, "My Father, if it be possible, let this cup pass from me; nevertheless, not as I will, but as you will." (Matt. 26:38–39)

Jesus takes His sorrow and places it at His Father's feet. He begs for change. And finally, He surrenders His will. In our confusion and exhaustion, we can look to Christ's example. He's never unclear about the power or priority of prayer, especially in His darkest moments.

For me, this comes as a huge relief. The call on our lives is lighter than we might think—and it's also lighter than we might even sometimes *prefer*. When we aren't personally doing something tangible, the situation can feel so out of control. But our prayers are commanded by God. Prayers are not a way for us to do something tangibly, yet they're the most important thing we can do.

So let's pray fervently and often for specific individuals, inviting other believers in our lives to pray as well. Pray with anyone who will bow their head with you. Bring the names of lost people before the Lord, and know that this service far surpasses any other work.

In online dating, I never liked the idea of "casting a wide net." But in prayer, I think the concept is apt. Spread the names of your lost loved ones far and wide: to your church, to your family members, and to your friends and neighbors. Invite them to intercede along with you for the salvation of your lost friends and family members. Ask them to continue asking the Lord eagerly and with great expectation.

It's hard for me to even contain my excitement when someone says to me, "I've been praying for Charlotte." Next time you have a conversation with another believer, ask them for a name too. What great joy we can find in praying specifically and consistently for people by name. What a grand privilege, indeed.

Reflection Room

Wrestle: Do you catch yourself spending more time worrying about the salvation of your loved ones than you do praying about it? God is inviting You into communion with Him in this waiting. Next time an eternal concern crosses your mind, go immediately to God in prayer. Consider practicing this habit daily.

Flee from Doubt

So here we are asking the Lord for change. And ... asking and asking and asking. And still asking. This can only mean one thing: it's time to talk about "ask fatigue."

Desire for other people's salvation is deep, but it can become dull from exhaustion, in much the same way I relentlessly use my lone kitchen knife, relying on it to get the job done without any care or upkeep. Sometimes my prayers for my lost friends get dull as well. They become worn out, as do I. Once when trying to describe the way that I was feeling in prayer, the words that came to mind were *ask fatigue*.

On the one hand, I became so good at praying all the right words so frequently that my heart wasn't participating—only my tongue. And on the other hand, when my heart *was* involved day after day for months on end, fatigue would strike anyway because, frankly, I was worn down from the emotional effort. This grief is a heavy burden.

For me, if left unchecked, the result of ask fatigue is unbelief. It creeps in without me even realizing. This is because I'm tempted to look back at the result of all my previous asking and see, from my limited perspective, that things still look the same. In those moments, I wonder why I think (or even why I *should* think) that circumstances would be any different tomorrow. Can you relate to this exhaustion?

When human reasoning joins forces with ask fatigue, it creates doubt. Doubt is flavorless, and it steals joy. Doubt is a vacuum cleaner for hope. It sucks it all up! And it leads to something even more dangerous.

Doubt sets the scene, and then unbelief enters, stage left.

When unbelief takes the stage, I realize that I've perhaps neglected the needs of my own heart. Rather than seeking first the kingdom of God for His glory, I might've been seeking after God to *do something I wanted done* as soon as possible.

Do you ever find yourself praying so deeply and so often for the people you love that you neglect asking God for His grace in your own life? We should continue asking Him to give us wisdom and discernment, to give us hope and peace, to teach us how to abide in Him, and to keep our hearts tender and childlike before Him so that we will not doubt His character.

When I start to feel a sense of doubt or exhaustion, I turn to the Psalms. I read the cries of other hurting hearts begging for God's presence and help. I follow the examples of those godly psalmists who, despite their weariness, kept their hearts tender before the Lord by going to Him in prayerful communion. They realized the importance of God's comfort and aid in crisis. They also realized the importance of their relationship with God—knowing and enjoying Him over and above their asks.

Reflection Room

Recall: Psalm 16. Consider praying through this psalm verse by verse. When you go to the Lord in prayer, ask Him to give you joy in His presence. Prioritize spending time with God to know and enjoy Him rather than to get something from Him. Reflect on the psalmist's observations in Psalm 16:11:

> You make known to me the path of life;
>   in your presence there is fullness of joy;
>   at your right hand are pleasures forevermore.

Confidence and Consistency

During long seasons of unanswered prayer, I experienced another symptom of ask fatigue: I started to wonder if God might be annoyed with me, hearing the same pleas over and over, for years on end. To be honest, this would sort of annoy me in a relationship—especially if my answer was "Not right now."

But my pastor assuaged these fears by sharing these words: "The boldest prayer you can pray is the prayer you've prayed a hundred times before."[2]

Those prayers are sometimes the hardest, aren't they? They are forged in stone and tears. They are the words we've placed on the altar a hundred times. We keep carrying them back.

With my pastor's short declaration, I realized that the Lord delights in every earnest, humble, broken intercession we bring before Him. He is never annoyed. Our prayers are *never* a burden to God. He is delighted with our consistency and our care. We are free, and in fact are invited, to continue praying for these lost people we love for as long as the Spirit prompts us. For as long as we feel the burden of prayer on their behalf, God welcomes the cries of our hearts.

Bearing my own brokenness in mind, there's one final pitfall I've discovered with my ask fatigue. It comes from that doubt that carves a path toward unbelief. It comes from that voice in my head that observes that nothing has changed and asks what the point is in continuing. In this exhaustion, I'm reminded to seek care for my own heart. But I'm also challenged by the belief that my asking would guarantee an answer on my timeline. *I'm tempted to elevate my action to a level of consequence on par with God's power.*

When I observe my own efforts in prayer and conclude that I have changed nothing and should consider stopping, that's pride. My pride suggests that something should have happened because I did something to make it happen. There is relief in the call to pray being an easy ask, and there is relief in God's invitation to our repeated cries. But there is even more relief in recognizing and accepting our own powerlessness.

Rather than feeling frustrated that our prayers do not, in and of themselves, accomplish our purpose (or God's purpose, for that matter), we can take great comfort that we ask and that *it is God* who answers. Our observations of the circumstances at hand are so extremely finite and limited that we should be glad that our prayers are not always granted: "For now we see in a mirror dimly" (1 Cor. 13:12a).

When we realize our powerless position in this devastating situation, we can all the better appreciate that God has given us this great mercy of direct communication with Him. We have a constant, open channel to speak with the Creator of the entire universe. And what's more, we're told He hears us. Meditating on this alone comforts an aching heart. It invites an awareness and acceptance of our own clouded view. It empowers us to keep begging, day after day, even for the exact same thing. And to keep surrendering, day after day, to the Lord's will.

I've experienced a few occasions in which my relationships with nonbelievers have become challenging and painful in ways that didn't feel fair or worth it. I have felt a degree of perpetual exhaustion as my life pointed me toward the Lord and their lives worshipped myriad things, from status to money to accomplishments. I wanted to walk away. I developed greater empathy for folks who run to their bubbles of faithful, God-fearing friends and stay there, despite the Great Commission.

But the exhaustion I was experiencing had less to do with the misguided focus of my lost loved ones and more to do with my own. I was tempted to focus on my own "perfect" witness in those relationships. I was tempted to concentrate only on things I felt I could control. I realized that I had been trying to manipulate God into doing my will rather than gladly serving His. But I can no more control God than an ant can control the weather.

> *God mercifully includes us in His work, and we have the privilege to sit beneath Him in the shadow of His love.*

I find it overwhelming to contemplate the authority and autonomy of the God of the universe. But when I keep in mind His perfect power and majesty as the One in control and when I direct my focus to His deep and unfailing love for me, suddenly my relational challenges begin to fall under His domain rather than mine. They shift from things I try to control to things I trust that He will handle in His timing and power according to His will.

It's this submission that so greatly relieves me from much of the relational anxiety as well. Genuine knowledge of God's love fosters relationship with Him through prayer and peace under His power. In this recognition, there is not burden but freedom. We don't control His answers, only the consistency with which we bring to Him our requests.

Reflection Room

Reframe: Instead of giving in to frustration from repeated and seemingly unanswered prayers, be reminded that your continued asking is an invitation from God to lean on Him and experience His love for you in your waiting. Rather than viewing your powerlessness as a limitation, rest in the unlimited power of the One who has called You to Himself with your prayers. Might God desire your praise, care, and affections in prayer to build relationship with Him so that He can carry your burdens?

Salvation Belongs to God

When we contemplate our diligence in praying for people we love, it's easy to think that we are playing some part, however small, in their salvation. As if we are doing 1 percent and God is handling the other 99 percent. But freedom is found in the awareness that God is doing all 100 percent. The effort and diligence that we bring sits outside the entirety of what God is accomplishing through His power and by His will. God mercifully includes us in His work, and we have the privilege to sit beneath Him in the shadow of His love.

We don't need to barter with God or try to split the labor or worry that we aren't doing our part. The pressure is off, and the responsibility and power rest with God alone. Our prayers have so much value—they draw us closer to the Lord, incline our hearts to His, and are precious in His sight. A heart inclined toward God is also primely positioned to be used by God. We do our friends a great service to go before Him every day, interceding on their behalf.

We should pray that God would align our hearts to His, shine a light in the dark places, and use us in His kingdom work. Though His love is not earned through our usefulness, we have the privilege of serving as the humble spoon on which a great delicacy is offered. We carry the news of His goodness. He is the portion, and we are simply the utensil sitting beneath. When you start to feel responsible for outcomes, remember, "Salvation belongs to the LORD!" (Jon. 2:9b).

As Spurgeon writes, "When you have done all, trust in God as though you had done nothing."[3]

Prayer Changes Our Hearts

How great is our privilege of prayer on behalf of our lost friends! In a world where we often feel powerless to help people, to combat injustice, and to effect actual change, how wonderful that the Lord has provided a way for us to directly intercede. There's no bureaucracy, no expense. We get to go before the God of the universe on behalf of people we know and love, and even people we don't know. There is no greater act of service.

But all our tangible efforts are mere pennies in comparison to the great riches of prayer. When the world seeks to help the world, it generally involves money, skills and expertise, or other resources. When I contemplate worldly service, I'm reminded of John 14:27, where Jesus says of the peace He offers, "Not as the world gives do I give to you."

In this same way, our greatest service to our lost friends might not look like the world's best offering. That's because it's not a worldly service but a heavenly commission: "Pray without ceasing" (1 Thess. 5:17). It's counterintuitive to what the world would say is valuable or even logical—to spend time communing with a heavenly being, to ask Him for help.

But don't be fooled by the world's logic. The specific people the Lord has placed in our lives and on our hearts are the very names He loves to hear when we cry out to Him in prayer. We have been placed in these relationships not only to love and serve these friends out of the overflow of God's love for us but even more so to intercede fervently and often on their behalf that the Lord might incline their hearts to His.

The specific people the Lord has placed in our lives and on our hearts are the very names He loves to hear when we cry out to Him in prayer.

This might seem like an easy option. You might be thinking, *That's not hard enough. I need to do more.* If so, I'd encourage you to spend even five minutes a day interceding for a specific lost loved one consistently for some period of time. I guarantee that doing this will challenge you. It will cause you to think deeply, to ask more questions, and even to wrestle. It will draw your heart closer to God's and align your will with His.

Over time, consistent prayer enables us to see the people we love the way God sees them. We begin to view people less as lost sheep without eternal identities and more as image bearers, fearfully and wonderfully made. If you're inclined to think it's easy or fruitless, give it a try and see what happens in your heart.

Reflection Room

Wrestle: Do you become discouraged when your prayers don't lead to circumstantial change? Do you find yourself more inclined to physical acts of service than prayerful intercession? When it comes to a loved one's salvation, might you occasionally find yourself inclined to the mantra "If you want something done right, do it yourself"? In what ways might you be able to fight the temptation to spend less time in prayer and instead prioritize interceding for your lost loved ones and even lost people around the world?

Image-Bearing Artistry

What strikes me most when I think of my friend Charlotte is her uniqueness. She is an original work of art for which there is no comparison. God has given her endearing and creative attributes that set her apart from everyone else. Such is the case for all the specific people in our lives for whom we're praying. Think of all the things you love about them. See the Creator's hand at work. How lovely, how marvelous are the works of God's hand—each and every one of them. Our worlds wouldn't look the same if even one were missing. Their very existence was ordained before the creation of time.

The Lord loves all our lost friends. They are, above all else, His children. When we cry out to Him in prayer, He delights in our pleadings, because He loves these *specific* individuals more than any of us ever could. More than we can possibly imagine. Believer, rest in the Lord's great, unending, unfailing love for your sweet friends and family. My prayer for all of us is not only that we will receive big miracles soon but also that we will remain steadfast in praise, even if we do not. He hears our every prayer, and He's always on the other end of the line listening. You're never cut off from His ear.

My church opened a new campus while I was writing this chapter. A few weeks before the grand opening, we met there in small groups to walk through each room and pray for what the Lord would do in that place. We walked through the nurseries, and we prayed for the children and for protection and fruitfulness in their lives. We walked through the classrooms, and we prayed for learning and understanding. We walked through the fellowship hall, and we prayed for relationship and connection. We ended in the sanctuary, where we begged God to save the lives of many in our city, and we prayed for Him to move powerfully in their hearts.

Finally, we took Sharpies to the concrete foundation, soon to be covered over in carpet, and we wrote the names of the people we desperately desired to see saved. I wrote Charlotte's name that day at the base of the column on the back-right side of the room. And then I knelt before the Lord and prayed that He would make His name great in Charlotte's life, that her life might glorify Him in the world.

There are hundreds of names written on that floor.

Prayer Starter

God, thank You for the mighty power of prayer. Thank You for the privilege of bringing the names of my lost friends before You. I am deeply humbled, Father, that You invite me to be involved in Your pursuit of their hearts. Through my interceding, please align my heart and will with Yours. When I am discouraged, please nudge me gently to bow my head before You, rather than to cast my cares elsewhere. Please deepen my relationship with You through my prayers, and let my focus be on You rather than solely on what I'm asking for. Please convict me when the things I want cast a shadow over who You are. I am thankful that salvation is Yours to offer.

Chapter 8

How Do I Wait Victoriously with This Sense of Urgency?

One of my favorite childhood movies is *Annie*. I can be a bit skeptical about the future, but Annie isn't. She's an image of hopefulness. In the classic movie song "Tomorrow," her character sings that tomorrow is never more than one day away. She loves tomorrow.

I think about tomorrows a lot. I hum the song's tune. Todays can feel dark in our waiting. I want to emulate Annie's hopefulness. I want to lean into the words of Charles Spurgeon, who writes, "You may say that today is black, but I say that tomorrow is coming."[1]

Tomorrow, though, by definition, never arrives. It's always just up ahead. And it often feels like that's where the answers to my prayers might be ... just out of reach. None of my todays have seen my loved ones saved.

So how do we keep waiting for all those tomorrows? And how do we wait in ways that are sustainable and God-honoring?

There's a vast expanse between just waiting and waiting well. I'll bet you know what I mean. You're waiting one way or another—there's no doubt about it. But maybe it's sucking the life out of you. It's probably caused quite a few of the thoughts and questions we've explored. Maybe you're feeling exhausted.

I know firsthand because I spent the better part of a few years waiting quite poorly. I'm intimately familiar with all the deep questions and discouraging thoughts I've addressed in earlier chapters because I've lived through them one by one—and often simultaneously.

Why is it so hard to wait well? And what does waiting well even look like?

One night while sharing takeout with Charlotte, a strange thought crossed my mind. Charlotte's senior-aged cat, Jack, was particularly affectionate that evening. He spent some time with us, enjoying our company. This was quite unusual, given Jack's often antisocial tendencies, and so I took notice and mused a bit over his life. Jack has struggled as he's aged, and it's clear that his time to leave this world is fast approaching. I took in his sweet tuxedo-shaded frame and noted his delicate features. Pets are a treasure of which I often feel unworthy.

I let my mind wander to my own memories with my senior cats, now passed on. I reveled in the thought of seeing them again. I began to imagine Charlotte's cat in heaven ... without her ... forever. I observed what great joy Jack experienced in Charlotte's presence—the only caregiver he's ever known. His affectionate and tender provider. The awarder of great love and careful protection for him. What if they were separated forever?

This was, admittedly, a fairly odd thought. In that moment, one conclusion weighed on me: *There's nothing I can do about it one way or another.*

I felt so empty, and I experienced the bitter awareness of my inability to enact change. There was nothing Jack could do about it either. It felt as though my only lot in life, at least within the context of this friendship, was to wait and see. No guarantees. No promises. I love Charlotte dearly. It's impossibly painful for me to consider an eternity without her.

It exposed again that sense of powerlessness, that most vulnerable challenge of waiting: the realization of our lack of control. The pain we feel takes on new depth when accompanied by the awareness of our own smallness. We might even feel a bit irrelevant. In that moment, I certainly looked into the face of my own uncomfortable dependency.

When we ruminate on our smallness, our finitude, and our total lack of control, waiting can feel like a void of hopelessness that threatens to consume our trust in a Father who loves us. So how do we wait well, in ways that are edifying to God, ourselves, and our loved ones?

We start by recognizing that our weakness reminds us that we are not God. That's a good thing. Paul tells us in 2 Corinthians 12 that our weakness is a gateway through which God's power and grace can enter our lives. This means that we can rejoice whenever we feel weak or powerless.

If dwelling on our lack of control steals hope, perhaps there's something far better to which we can turn our attention. I've found that there are three ways to wait that lead us to reap joy and deepen our trust in God rather than be shipwrecked on an island of our own inadequacy.

We can wait with open hands.

We can wait while meditating on God's promises.

And we can wait by worshipping.

Let's explore these.

Reflection Room

Recall: Psalm 147. Does recognition of your own smallness discourage you? Reflect on the Lord's unlimited power, and remember that you serve a God who sees all the details and fills in all the gaps. Pray through this psalm, praising God for His authority and asking Him for rest in His strength. Consider committing Psalm 147:4–5 to memory:

> He determines the number of the stars;
>> he gives to all of them their names.
> Great is our Lord, and abundant in power;
>> his understanding is beyond measure.

Release Our Grasp

About ten years ago, I developed a strong friendship and deep care for another nonbelieving friend. I was a government intern at the time, enjoying all that my city had to offer with none of the cares and concerns of endless work life. Those were the days.

That summer, I was assigned to sit next to a fellow intern named Katelyn. After sitting next to her every day for the roughly ten-week internship, we became quite close. I was twenty years old at the time, and having not truly decided to follow Christ until sometime after high school, this was really the first time I had developed such a deep care for the condition of someone's heart.

Katelyn was vibrant, unapologetic, enthusiastic, and funny. She was one of the least judgmental people I'd ever met and was a joy to be around. I wanted Katelyn to know Jesus. It seemed to me they could be great friends. I prayed earnestly for her that summer, and I memorized 1 Corinthians 13:4–8. To this day, I can recite the full passage immediately and with ease. And whenever I do, I am reminded of some of the most encouraging words I've encountered on my journey of waiting: *Love is patient.*

That summer internship seems like it was a lifetime ago. It has, after all, been more than a decade. And as for Katelyn? I am still patiently waiting for this sweet friend to follow Jesus.

Over the years, I've prayed often that God would give me the trust to submit Katelyn's heart to Him. In walking through the last ten years of waiting for this friend, God has shown me the first way in which we can wait well. *We wait by relinquishing control.* By submitting our desires and our plans to the ultimate Planner.

We wait with open hands.

I've got a tendency to grasp tightly the things for which my heart deeply longs. To be honest, in some situations, there's been more pain in loosening my grasp than in receiving an answer of no.

The summer after meeting Katelyn, I applied for my dream internship. It was everything I thought I'd wanted since I was twelve. I'd set my sights on the place, and I was very determined. But then came the unexpected hurdle.

The interview process did not go as well as I'd expected. I walked away crushed and quite sure I had ruined it all. I needed to get away and think things through. I was only in college. How had it all already gone so wrong? How could I lose this thing I'd wanted so badly, looked forward to for so long? I had been patiently waiting. It felt cruel.

I drove a few hours to the coast and booked a cheap hotel. I spent the weekend deep in thought, wandering down windswept, deserted beaches. It was March. I was still young in my faith and didn't quite know how to cope with this loss. I didn't know how to open my hands before the Lord. But He was kind and gentle with me. He whispered to me that my career was His and that I needed to relinquish control. I had held this dream so tightly that even the thought of its loss threatened to crush my soul, grinding it to dust. God didn't want me to live that way. He wanted me to trust Him with my life.

At the end of the weekend, after begging God to help me, through choked sobs and the pain of impending loss, I genuinely surrendered my dream to the Lord. I let it go completely. I loosened my grasp and set it before Him. I told the Lord, This is Yours now, and I trust You with it. This might seem dramatic for a college internship. But to me, it was my world.

The heart posture of surrender before the Lord is the birthing room of trust.

What strikes me upon reflection is that even though I told the Lord that I was giving Him my plans, they had been His all along. I might've let go of my dream, but it's humbling to reflect on the fact that it was never mine to begin with. We can't let go of things that were never ours to grasp. But we can certainly surrender. The heart posture of surrender before the Lord is the birthing room of trust. How the Lord deeply loves our genuine surrender before Him. He wants to meet us there and gently help us through the process.

In the end, I actually did get the job. It was the best summer of my life. It was an exhilarating, whirlwind few months. I soaked it all in. I loved the people, the work, the environment. I never did get hired there permanently, though that had been my goal. That's a dream I'll never realize, and I've mourned the loss. But you know what? The mourning process for what I lost was greatly eased by the Lord's mercy in having had me surrender it to Him already.

My mourning was laced with deep gratitude that He'd let me get a glimpse inside that place. He let me go in and look around and enjoy the place, even if only for a few months. I'm so thankful for that summer. My memories of living out a dream will last a lifetime, as will the friends I made there. But I can't imagine what greater sorrow I would've experienced had the Lord not been gracious enough to show me how to release my dream into His hands early on.

Because of His mercy, I was able to enjoy the summer in total freedom. I wasn't worried about getting back there in the future—or about the possibility that it might not happen. I got to just show up and enjoy the gift. No pressure. No expectation. I had released my grip. The job was set in my open palms before Him. So, when it was taken

later, I wasn't desperately trying to claw it back—I was just grateful to
have known it at all.

Releasing the heart of a person to God is certainly different from
releasing a career aspiration. It is much heavier, far more eternally
consequential. But God wants to meet us even in that place and help
us hold our desires loosely before Him. He wants to show us deep
mercy as we open our hands. He wants us to enjoy freedom in our
relationships with our friends and family members—to love them
deeply and without desperate grasping over what we'd like to see
happen in their lives.

Reflection Room

Reframe: Instead of fighting for control, either in actions
or in attitude, recognize that salvation is a divine, gracious
gift, already far removed from any work of yours. But rather
than mentally preparing for the worst, open your heart to
receive God's gentle comfort and meditate on Lamentations
3:22–24:

> The steadfast love of the LORD never ceases;
>   his mercies never come to an end;
> they are new every morning;
>   great is your faithfulness.
> "The LORD is my portion," says my soul,
>   "therefore I will hope in him."

Rest in His Promises

I have experienced brief stretches of time during which I've felt content, waiting hopefully on the Lord with confidence in His faithfulness. But then I'll ask myself, *Why should I have peace when the eternity of people I love is unsure? The audacity of me! How dare I carry on with a joyful life, even as my loved ones meander aimlessly toward destruction!*

In those moments, the Enemy finds a foothold of doubt in my mind and moves in, taking up full residence to exploit my fear about my friends' eternal destinations. Rather than rejoicing over this gift of peace from God, I've let the Enemy get the best of me, leading me to believe that I shouldn't have peace in a situation like this.

In these moments, Galatians 5:1 reminds me to stand firm and not submit to this yoke of slavery all over again. Peace is one of Jesus's primary gifts to His children, through His Spirit within us.

Make no mistake, though—the Devil is your enemy. He will steal or poison even the fruit of the Spirit. Have you ever caught him trying to do the same to you?

On one hand, the Enemy roots for the death and destruction of our loved ones. And on the other hand, he wants to consume us with worry about their salvation—all while plotting against them!

The Enemy's aim is to consume us, to drown out the promises of God and the truth of His great love for our friends and family. The Enemy doesn't care about our loved ones. Despite causing us to worry about the souls of the people we love, he is fully against us and them. The worst mistake in the world would be to listen to anything he is saying. We cannot trust him or let him steal our awareness of God's goodness. He is against us.

But God is for us.

In these moments of stolen peace and misdirection by the Enemy, God has reminded me to meditate on His promises.

This is the second way in which we can wait well: we can remind ourselves of the promises of God.

We memorize them. We dwell on them. We live in recognition of them. And when we're distracted or feel that we shouldn't have peace, we remind ourselves of the promises all the more. We remember that these distractions are lies from God's lesser adversary. These are lies from an Enemy who seeks only to steal, kill, and destroy (John 10:10).

Not only can we remind ourselves of the promises of God, but we can also take refuge in them. His Word is a hiding place of deep comfort. He is the provider of peace and the author of goodness. He seeks not to kill or destroy but to give abundant life and life everlasting (John 3:16).

When it comes to the salvation of our friends, we don't have guarantees and we don't have sure promises. But in God's deep love for us, we have even better promises, as shown in Jesus's words in Matthew 6:

> And why do you worry about clothes? See how the flowers of the field grow. They do not labor or spin. Yet I tell you that not even Solomon in all his splendor was dressed like one of these. If that is how God clothes the grass of the field, which is here today and tomorrow is thrown into the fire, will he not

much more clothe you—you of little faith? So do not worry, saying, "What shall we eat?" or "What shall we drink?" or "What shall we wear?" For the pagans run after all these things, and your heavenly Father knows that you need them. But seek first his kingdom and his righteousness, and all these things will be given to you as well. Therefore do not worry about tomorrow, for tomorrow will worry about itself. Each day has enough trouble of its own. (vv. 28–34 NIV)

When you start to believe the Enemy's lies, remember:

- God promises that He will provide for our needs (Phil. 4:19).
- God promises that pain will end and that relief is coming, if only in eternity (Ps. 23; 2 Cor. 4:17–18; Rev. 21:4).
- God promises that He will be with us, no matter what (Josh. 1:9).

When we take refuge in the truth that our God is good, that He's looking out for us, that He's with us, and that He's working to end pain and suffering once and for all, we can trust Him with the places in our hearts that are hurting. We can go to His Word and let Him show us who He is and how much He loves us.

Reflection Room

Request: Father, please protect me from the lies of the Enemy. Thank You for Your good promises. When my peace is threatened, please bring Your Word to mind. Give me discipline to commit to memory passages that the Spirit may use to comfort me in my distress. When I've wandered off in forests of doubt, let Your promises pull me back to Your peace.

Rejoice Always

Do you ever let your mind wander into the world of fantasy? I'll sometimes find myself imagining moments when my loved ones recognize their separation from Christ, repent of their sins, and submit their lives to the Lord of the universe. I imagine falling to my knees in tearful praise, worship abounding for my God. Maybe you also have an active imagination.

One evening, I began to invent salvation scenarios for all my lost friends. I planned out many ways that God could save them. I imagined the depth of my worship before the Lord when He finally gave me what I'd been seeking. But deep within one of these fictional journeys, it suddenly occurred to me: there was no need to wait ... I could live this way *right now*.

Instead of storing up my worship for when I received the objects of my desire, I could walk through my daily grieving by worshipping the Lord now. I could choose fervent, faithful worship in the face of deep and unrelenting sorrow. Prayerful, powerful (and probably tearful) worship as a response to pain.

Such is the third way we wait well; we wait by worshipping.

Worship delights the Lord. Scripture is rich with directives to worship (Ps. 69:34; Isa. 12:5; Luke 4:8; Heb. 13:15). For me, worship often takes the form of praise through song. The Bible is also full of instructions to praise God through singing and rejoicing (Ps. 71:23; 100:1–2; Jer. 20:13).

Sometimes, my worship is energetic and encouraged. But other times, when I'm brought low with sorrow, I confess that I just don't feel like blasting cheerful tunes. If you have days when your heart also feels heavy, you can still choose to worship. Over time, we can turn our purposeful decisions to worship into habits of praise.

No matter how we worship, we can train our hearts to do so habitually. Then, when distress overtakes us, we will automatically flee to the arms of our Father. We see an example of worship during distress in Acts 16. Paul and Silas are imprisoned for casting out an evil spirit in the name of Jesus. They have rarely been weaker, and yet they know this means God's power is strong in them. They don't know if God will intervene or not, but the two prisoners are worshipping.

> About midnight Paul and Silas were praying and singing hymns to God, and the prisoners were listening to them, and suddenly there was a great earthquake, so that the foundations of the prison were shaken. And immediately all the doors were opened, and everyone's bonds were unfastened. (vv. 25–26)

We may be living in a situation that feels very much like a prison. It is dark. There seems to be no escape. No freedom. No strength. We can follow Paul's lead and worship anyway. When upbeat worship music feels wrong, I'll turn on Horatio Spafford's "It Is Well with My Soul" or another hymn that points to the peace of God. We can soak in the words. We can lift our voices to our Deliverer.

We can worship on our knees in prayer. We can worship in the quietness of our hearts as we carry out our daily chores. We can worship in song and dance. When we have a worshipping heart, we can look at all the things that hurt and don't make sense and say, "God fills the gap." A worshipping heart turns to the Lord and says, "You are enough." It also has a way of taking our eyes off our own circumstances and refocusing them on the Lord.

I can't always jump up and down to energetic praise music. Sometimes, all I can do is mouth Spafford's words:

> *When peace like a river attendeth my way,*
> *When sorrows like sea-billows roll,*
> *Whatever my lot, Thou has taught me to know;*
> *It is well, it is well with my soul.*[2]

Even our humblest worship delights the Lord—especially when it's all we have to give. In our worship, we embody Psalm 23:1. I'm particularly fond of the New Living Translation, which reads,

> The LORD is my shepherd;
> I have all that I need.

Reflection Room

> **Wrestle:** Brainstorm a few ways you might incorporate acts of personal worship into your daily routine. Whether it's praying, singing along with worship music, journaling, or any other form of praise, what habits might you begin to develop to present your thanksgiving to God?

Surrender Our Will

Despite my imagined salvation scenarios for Charlotte and all my other loved ones, as of this writing, none of them have come to fruition. I'm not, after all, the author of their stories.

In observing how fruitless my proposed plans are at controlling the narrative, I sometimes also glimpse my unwillingness to relinquish control—to wait with open hands and a worshipful spirit that trusts in God's promises. On several occasions, I've prayed to the Lord, "Please save Your daughter Charlotte, no matter what it takes." I'm guessing we've all prayed something like this over our lost friends.

But once, after including this request in my evening prayers, a distressing question came to mind: *What if all it takes is simply the passing of time?* Horrified, I remember thinking, *Wait a second—no! That's not what I meant. Anything but that! What I meant was that I want You to save Charlotte now, no matter what, in one of these ways I've planned, or in any way, really. But not twenty years down the road ... So, yes, whatever it takes, as long as it's on my timeline.*

Of course, this was not my response in so many words. But it was my mind's inclination. Upon asking the Lord to save my friend regardless of the cost, I remember my feeling of shock realizing that the cost could be a few more decades. Whether consciously or not, I'm daily making plans for how things should play out. Even if God doesn't reveal Himself through divine revelation or personal struggle or any of the other potential means that I've concocted, I've still got my preferred timeline in mind ... if not today, then at least by next month.

We'd probably be delighted to accept any of our imagined salvation scenarios. It doesn't matter which one. So perhaps it doesn't seem like a control issue on the surface. But when we consider what God's timing might be, our desire to maintain control rears its head. Our disappointment appears a bit more vividly. We don't care how the thing is done, but we'd like it done sooner rather than later.

Waiting isn't merely testing or trial; it's paving the way for intimacy with God. In relationship with the Father, there is great reward.

We are sometimes maintaining a tighter grasp than we realize—not out of any sort of purposeful disobedience but more out of the fear that we could be waiting a very, very long time. It's not necessarily this feeling of apprehension that is the cause for concern but rather what we choose to do with it. Will we keep demanding that God fit our timelines, or will we submit to Him our worries, the things on which our minds meditate, and the posture of our hearts?

As C. S. Lewis aptly writes, "Nothing that you have not given away will ever really be yours."[3] This feels all the more true when it comes to our plans, dreams, and deep desires for the salvation of the people we love. But true freedom and unencumbered joy in the waiting are found in an unexpected place: total submission of our plans to our Father, who loves us.

When we truly give up something we deeply long for, to get it back is joy, and to get something else instead may bring equal joy, for neither thing was ours to begin with. As we lay down the things we long for, we may mourn for a time. But when we submit to God the things we want, we can say assuredly:

> I remain confident of this:
> I will see the goodness of the LORD
> in the land of the living. (Ps. 27:13 NIV)

In prayer, I asked God why this journey toward Charlotte's freedom had to be so hard-fought. If God was planning to save her, why couldn't He just do it already? Why must you and I be placed in these long seasons of painful waiting?

But then something occurred to me. I thought about my reaction whenever I hear that someone I don't know has chosen to follow Jesus. For example, I hear the testimonies of other church members, listen to pastoral accounts of heart change, and read newsletters with stories

of repentance. In all these instances, I rejoice and have much gladness over their salvation. I'm sure you do as well. We thank God for revealing the truth to them, and we celebrate a shared eternal inheritance. It's a wonderful thing to witness. Yet, we're still waiting for that day of soulful celebration for our loved ones.

Imagine the excitement of celebrating that salvation—of hearing that loved one's testimony after many years of prayer. Such a deep, unbridled overflow of joy is hardly imaginable. How sweet, how rich, and how merciful that moment would be. We might not even have words. And why is that?

Because God made us wait with a heart posture surrendered to His will.

> *Waiting well gives us freedom, and freedom allows us to show up in the lives of our people without the weight of their salvation resting on our shoulders.*

In the waiting, He hasn't left us alone or burdened us with pointless pain. Rather, *He's involved us.* He's included us in His pursuit. How exceedingly merciful that God is inviting us into His plans. How indescribably kind that the Lord would let us take part in the work He is doing. Even while we remember that we don't control the outcome, how rich is God's love for us that He lets us converse with Him daily about the people we love—and that He shares our love for them as image bearers.

If I do see the salvation of my close friends and family, how much more will I fall to my knees and worship a God who let me go alongside Him in search of them? In this way, waiting isn't merely testing or trial; it's paving the way for intimacy with God. In relationship with the Father, there is great reward.

Learning to wait well doesn't just make things easier for us. It also glorifies God and honors our loved ones. Waiting well gives us freedom, and freedom allows us to show up in the lives of our people without the weight of their salvation resting on our shoulders. We could never successfully carry that load, anyway. Believe me, I've tried.

We can wait well when we know that, ultimately, our victory is won. We have challenges and pain in this life, but we know how it ends. We've read the last chapter of the Book, and we know who wins. We can live victoriously in the knowledge that good triumphs over evil.

Even so, we're still left with our question: Are our friends and family on the winning team? We may not get this answer soon. But hope, hope, hope in the Lord and His timing, that He may one day, perhaps even tomorrow, draw our sweet friends and family close to Him. Do not hope in their salvation. Hope in the God who saves. Hope with open hands, a mind focused on His promises, and a heart that continually rejoices in worship. Praise Him today, and remember: tomorrow is coming.

Prayer Starter

God, I'm so thankful that You are the perfect Author of reality. You are in control. Thank You for Your good promises. You alone, Lord, are worthy of my praise. Please help me wait with open hands before You. Give me freedom in my waiting by helping me surrender my will to Yours. When I am hurting, please remind me of Your steadfast promises. Please whisper them to me in quiet moments. Let me develop a habit of worship that enables me to run to You in my pain, rather than to worldly distractions. Thank You for letting me come with You in pursuit of people I love. Help me trust in Your timeline and wait in ways that honor them well. Lord, please show me Your goodness in the land of the living.

Chapter 9

What Role Does My Faith Play in Their Salvation?

"The general ledger software is malfunctioning. An expense account was miscategorized, the balance sheet isn't balancing, and we can't close the year-end books. The auditors will be here in an hour!"

I needed help. After a perfect storm of departures, I ended up playing the role of accounting manager after only about four months on the job in my first corporate accounting role. I was putting out fires as quickly as I could, but the software management piece was new to me.

My supervisor replied, "So what's your proposed solution?"

Tremble in fear, I thought. *Confess to the auditors that I have no idea what I'm doing. Run away!* Instead, though, I rambled off a few options that felt like reasonable starting points, and much to my surprise, my boss seemed pleased. She agreed to help me take a look at some account classifications and figure out what we needed to do in the system.

Thank goodness, it was all worked out by the time the audit team arrived. We found an analytical solution to the problem, and I was able to contribute even more than I thought.

I love clean solutions. I even love spreadsheets—so much. You might say I *excel* at problem-solving (pun intended).

Sometimes I think we're tempted to view our faith like that too—as a solution to a problem rather than a relationship of trust. It's not a hard trap to fall into. Our mental archetype for how to handle problems is to *solve* them rather than submit them to someone else.

A relationship of faith sometimes challenges our natural inclinations.

I've found myself trying to throw my faith at my problems. I want it to move mountains. But what if rather than moving mountains, my faith keeps them standing still? Could my faith impact the people around me? Could it hurt them?

Maybe you've read Matthew 21:21, as I did, and worried about the role your faith might play in the lives of your loved ones.

> And Jesus answered them, "Truly, I say to you, if you have faith and do not doubt, you will not only do what has been done to the fig tree, but even if you say to this mountain, 'Be taken up and thrown into the sea,' it will happen."

I've studied the context of this verse and understand its intent as hyperbole or exaggeration. And yet, since so many biblical stories are about faith alone, I've often wondered how my faith comes into play, especially in my evangelistic work. I admit a few rudimentary thoughts have occurred to me while pondering these questions. Perhaps you've wondered these things too:

- Am I somehow contributing to my loved ones' separation from God?
- Or, if not directly contributing to the situation itself, am I still failing to help "fix" it?
- If I knew the Lord better, would He hear me and answer?
- What responsibility do I bear in all of this?
- Where is the end of me and the beginning of God?

Perhaps it's apparent to you from our journey together so far that pain has a way of taking our eyes off God and casting our focus back on ourselves. In isolated moments here and there, there's nothing necessarily wrong with this. We're allowed to feel and acknowledge pain and even sit with it for a while as we process the things that are happening in our lives. This is what it is to be human. But in intense affliction, I've found it hard to take my focus off myself and direct my eyes back to God. Simply put, sometimes it's hard to see past myself. And looking to myself for answers, assurance, or hope has, of course, failed dramatically.

Lately, I'm praying that the Lord would allow me to think of myself less—not that I would necessarily think less of myself but simply that my thoughts would focus more on God and others and less on me. "He must increase, but I must decrease" (John 3:30).

I don't want to get in God's way. And when I'm not the center of my focus, my problems seem smaller, as I'm focused on God's sovereignty over my own ability. When I'm not at the center, I experience much greater freedom. Healthy selflessness based on the security of knowing who we are as children of God is a path to deep joy. Seeing past ourselves lets us see more clearly the divine majesty of the God of the universe.

In my free time, I'm involved in the performing arts world. My artistic discipline is really just a hobby, but it keeps my mind engaged. The folks I'm with in that space make up a large portion of my regular community. I love these people, and so rather than always focusing on my performance, I try to show up and bring my most humble attitude. Candidly, it's a more relaxed, less competitive version of me than the urban business professional I turn into by day. I try not to take it—or myself—too seriously. I'm there to have a good time, improve my craft, and love others. I'd like to imagine I'm quite good at bringing the humor as well.

Of course, I'm not always successful. I have off days when I'm overly frustrated and self-critical … and not shy about it either. But the goal is to take the losses with the victories.

> Our loved ones are not hostages in a narrative that revolves around us and the strength of our faith.

I had a bad performance one day. I was able to laugh it off, realizing that my hobby is one step forward, three steps back. I was with the people I loved doing the thing I loved, and that was what mattered. I focused particularly hard on not bringing others down with my bad attitude. This was their activity too. Rather than being ashamed of my performance, I felt light and joyful afterward, and the

Lord spoke clearly to my heart, illuminating an important lesson: *When I'm able to realize that not everything is all about me, it really takes the pressure off.*

Oddly, this was a revelation I'd never stopped to consider. Rather than dwelling on my performance, I focused on showing up well for the community I loved. I fought for humility and patience and asked God to help grow those things in me rather than ruminating on my failures, dragging others down in the process. When I wasn't as focused on myself, I wasn't as concerned about my appearance. My performance didn't seem to matter as much as the joy of being with my people. This wasn't just about me. The pressure was off.

This makes sense in light of 1 Corinthians 13:4–8, the "love passage," as it's often called.

> Love is patient, love is kind. It does not envy, it does not boast, it is not proud. It does not dishonor others, it is not self-seeking, it is not easily angered, it keeps no record of wrongs. Love does not delight in evil but rejoices with the truth. It always protects, always trusts, always hopes, always perseveres.
>
> Love never fails. But where there are prophecies, they will cease; where there are tongues, they will be stilled; where there is knowledge, it will pass away. (NIV)

We can pray often that the Lord would grow in us the fruit of the Spirit outlined in this passage. Even where our performance doesn't measure up, we can show up and love well. Love does not envy, and it is not self-seeking.

We can draw some parallels here to our questions surrounding the salvation of our friends and family members. *Once we realize it's not all about us, it really takes the pressure off.* To put it more bluntly: our loved ones are not hostages in a narrative that revolves around us and the strength of our faith.

We are allowed to be works in progress. We're called to show up. By the grace of God, we're not expected to be perfect. Thank goodness—because we would fail every time. No one would be saved if salvation relied on us alone.

Reflection Room

Wrestle: Is your relationship with God ever distracted by your concern over showing up perfectly? He desires to commune with you and to know you, with however much faith you can bring moment by moment. Consider areas of fear or doubt in your relationships where a focus on perfection might be inhibiting you from showing up well and in ways that reflect trust in God.

Salvation Takes Away Shame

Questions about the role of our faith might be rooted in a place we least expect: guilt. Maybe it's guilt over our lack of consistent faith or guilt over our God choosing us to know Him. There might also be guilt over all the ways we could be doing more. Praying more. Fasting more. Serving more. Inviting more. Sharing more. If only we could just do, be, and say more. This guilt can leave us existing in endless cycles of rumination over our shortcomings.

In some ways, these feelings are accurate. We *are* guilty. We are guilty of sin before a holy God. Evil permeates our very being. We will never achieve any standard of perfection. It will remain that way on this side of heaven. And yet, salvation removes this guilt that we hold. Jesus's atoning sacrifice removes our sin as far as the east is from the west. We are reconciled to God, and we are cleansed by the righteous blood of Christ. His act is final and compensatory. Ironically, I sometimes feel guilt over my salvation. It's wrong, I know, especially since our salvation is what has rid us of guilt. Salvation takes away the shame of our insufficiency.

John 1:29 says it all: "The next day John saw Jesus coming toward him and said, 'Look, the Lamb of God, who takes away the sin of the world!'" (NIV).

Jesus covers us with His blood. Whatever weaknesses and insufficiencies we have, be it of love or faith or perseverance, He covers us. The Lord sees us in our lack and meets us with His abundance. He meets us in our shame and tells us that we don't bear the weight of perfection.

My faith *is* sometimes insufficient. Certainly, a sin for which I frequently repent is unbelief. Recall the Scripture we explored about the father asking for his son's healing. This unbelief, for me, often translates to anxiety over areas of life in which I'm holding on to something too tightly. So I ask God for forgiveness. In doing so, I also ask Him to free my mind from worrying over uncertainty.

To be human is to be uncertain. It's to be weak and limited and without the ability to control big things. But that's exactly where God wants us. Paul finds this out when he asks the Lord three times to grant a certain prayer (2 Cor. 12). Jesus finally tells him that He isn't ever going to grant Paul's prayer because being in that place of human powerlessness puts Paul in a position to experience God's power flowing through him.

God wants us in that same place. We hate our powerlessness and want it to end. But if we can experience God's resurrection power in our weakness, we might find ourselves more willing to sit in it and more watchful for what He will do.

It's not wrong to recognize the smallness of our faith, the resulting unbelief, and the impact it has on our lives. We are guilty. But God's grace is sufficient for us. It is freely offered and covers us completely, if only we ask for and accept it.

In desiring salvation for our friends, we would be wise to recognize the salvation God has given to *us*. Any guilt we feel has already been removed. Christ's sacrifice covers us. We can take hold of this truth in the same way we want our friends and family members to experience it.

Reflection Room

Reframe: Instead of viewing your own gift of salvation from God as a requirement to show up perfectly in the lives of your lost loved ones, be reminded that salvation is from God alone through faith alone (Eph. 2:8). Rather than experiencing pressure in our position, you and I can rest in God's ability to show up mercifully and miraculously in the lives of our lost friends and family. Might God desire your genuine heart, your praise, and your love more than the demonstration of your perfect faith in all circumstances?

Darkness to Light

In this chapter, we're exploring what role our faith might play in the salvation of our loved ones. Such a question might arise from another place besides guilt. It's the ground in which sorrow breeds and forms the beginnings of doubt. The place I'm speaking of is grief.

Grief, that miry pit of gloom that overtakes reason, chokes out joy, blinds hope, and blurs out the light. When I ask the question posed at the beginning of this chapter—when I start to wonder if my loved ones' salvation somehow rests on the shoulders of my faith—I do wade through the waters of guilt. But when I remind myself of my own salvation, which takes my guilt away, I can talk myself off the ledge.

The feeling of grief, though, may linger. Our salvation removes our guilt, but it may not entirely remove our grief.

When we wonder if people's salvation may somehow rely on us, sometimes it's because we're choosing to carry a weight of guilt that the Lord has already lifted. But other times, it's a question we're asking from a place of despair and desperation because we are deeply grieving. Sometimes, instead of worrying *if* our friends' salvation relies on us, we let our grief make us wish it *did*—because at least then, we might be able to do something about it.

We've talked about service, and we've talked about prayer. We're remarkably familiar with our own feelings of helplessness. So when we're already praying, already serving, already doing our best to wait well, what do we do with the grief that remains as our constant, prodding companion? There are moments when it might not be possible to put this concern out of our minds. It's okay to carry it wisely. But how do we do that practically?

Now that we have a foundation of waiting well, I'd like to revisit the concept of lament introduced at the beginning of our journey.

Every few months, as if on a schedule, I'm brought low with grief for the lost people I love. I take a few weeks and venture back through the Psalms. Many psalmists were experiencing deep sorrow as well, and I commune with them. I bring their same cries to the Lord who listens.

I'm reminded of the cries in Psalm 6:

> My soul is in deep anguish.
>   How long, LORD, how long? (v. 3 NIV)

And later:

> I am worn out from my groaning.
>
> All night long I flood my bed with weeping
>   and drench my couch with tears.
> My eyes grow weak with sorrow;
>   they fail because of all my foes. (vv. 6–7 NIV)

And then there's Psalm 25:

> Relieve the troubles of my heart
> and free me from my anguish. (v. 17 NIV)

A description I often use to capture the depth of my affliction over the eternities of lost people I love is "anguish of soul."

You might feel the same way. In the Psalms, it's clear we're not alone. Page after page of desperate pleading. Pages of sorrow, anguish, agony, despair. The psalmists are often facing different issues, and yet their words accurately reflect my torment. They understand me. And so, I look to them as examples for what I should do and how I should respond. They are lampposts on my narrow path. I embrace what often comes next from their lips to God's ear.

The psalmists take their pain to God. While they may sit with their pain for a little while, God meets them where they are. He doesn't expect them to get over it, brush it off, or push it aside. He's with them. He upholds them in His strength. And they know it.

> The LORD has heard my cry for mercy;
> the LORD accepts my prayer. (Ps. 6:9 NIV)

I like Psalm 18, in particular:

> In my distress I called to the LORD;
> I cried to my God for help.
> From his temple he heard my voice;
> my cry came before him, into his ears....

He reached down from on high and took hold of me;
he drew me out of deep waters....

You, LORD, keep my lamp burning;
my God turns my darkness into light. (Ps. 18:6, 16,
28 NIV)

And finally, there's Psalm 25:21, in which David cries,

May integrity and uprightness protect me,
because my hope, LORD, is in you. (NIV)

Notice how David doesn't focus on himself. He focuses squarely on God. We are allowed to sit alone with our pain. It's not wrong to take a moment to process. But lament takes our pain to God. Lament doesn't extinguish pain, but it removes us from experiencing our burdens in isolation. The Lord hears us, and He is always listening.

The biggest display of faith in our lives is when we acknowledge our deep, unbridled pain and instead of running away from our Father, we carry it all to the cross. Our faith won't save the people we love, but it certainly takes the focus off ourselves and glorifies God in the process. *Our faith itself is the very acknowledgment that God, rather than us, is the one who saves.*

By far the best resource I've found on grief, lament, and suffering in a broken world, apart from the Bible, is *Dark Clouds, Deep Mercy: Discovering the Grace of Lament* by Mark Vroegop. It's a book I'd recommend to every believer. It's preparation for affliction. It's instruction in sorrow. It's comfort in the deepest of grief. Vroegop understands suffering. He is all too familiar with wrestling. He knows that grief is, in his words, "vicious."[1] In the very first instruction on prayer, he writes, "Lament is a prayer in pain that leads to trust."[2] And later, "It is the path from heartbreak to hope."[3]

Our faith itself is the very acknowledgment that God, rather than us is the one who saves.

In wrestling with our questions of uncertainty and inadequacy, and even in trying to grapple with what feels like God's silence in our situation, we can lament, looking at our struggle and saying, "I will not walk through this wilderness alone but rather with God. His love for me covers my unanswered questions, even if I don't understand."

Vroegop writes:

> Life is full of vexing questions related to God's purposes. Pain often highlights perplexing paradoxes. Lament is expressed even though the tension remains. It turns to God in prayer, vocalizes the complaint, asks boldly, and chooses to trust while uncertainty hangs in the air. Lament doesn't wait for resolution. It gives voice to the tough questions before the final chapter is written.
>
> Lament is a journey through the shock and awe of pain.[4]

Try as I might, I've never reaped peace on the journey alone. Only in taking our pain to the feet of the Father can we receive the comfort of His presence. He is waiting to receive us. He knows.

Reflection Room

Request: Father, when I'm overwhelmed by the weight of circumstances around me, draw near to me. Remind me to run to You when grief darkens my view. Thank You that my loved ones are not reliant on me for the hope of their salvation. And yet, even in recognition of my helplessness, there is pain. As I grapple with the strength of my own faith, help me run to You with my questions, just as the psalmists do. Let me follow their example as I bring to You my grief and my total dependence.

Mustard Seeds and Mercy

While working through my faith's role in the circumstances I saw around me, I took a rideshare home from a friend's house. As soon as I sat down, I recognized my favorite worship music broadcast from my city's Christian radio station. This is somewhat of a rideshare rarity where I live, so I was excited and exclaimed, "Ah, my favorite radio station!" This elicited an equally surprised reaction from my driver. He said he most commonly gets asked, often angrily, to turn it off. He gets about one in fifty riders a week who delights in hearing music praising God.

We chatted about our faith, and he told me that he and his wife were fasting while in earnest prayer for the state of the world. They were praying for direction from God for our country's leaders, a revival of faith in our city and nation, and a turn from the pervasive wickedness in the world. But then he told me that he truly believed the problems in the world could be solved if everyone had deep and abiding faith. He said that if all repented and turned from their wicked ways and submitted their paths to the Lord, wars could be avoided, suffering would be greatly diminished, and peace would be completely restored.

It was a lengthier ride home, so we conversed on that topic for a few more minutes. We both had no doubt about how much suffering could be avoided if only the whole world followed Jesus. We both believed that faith was a doorway to peace. And yet, another reality came swiftly to mind: *no matter how much faith we have, sometimes God's answer to our prayers is no.*

We live in a shattered world. We are all rebels at heart (Gen. 8:21). Even in a faith-filled world, there is still sin, and there is still brokenness.

Faith is certainly strengthened when we see evidence of God working in our lives. It is a wonderful thing to see a prayer answered. But the reality is that if we base our faith entirely on God's answers to our prayers always being yes, we will quickly sink into deep doubt and emotional ruin. After all, the Lord said no to Paul, Peter, and pretty much every other Christian who has ever lived. God even refused to grant Jesus's prayer that His cup might be taken (Mark 14:36).

My discussion with my God-fearing driver that evening was encouraging. We were both praying for healing, for revival, and for the triumph of good over evil. And we were both reminded that the strength of our faith will not thwart God's plan or His timing. Even the strongest faith on earth won't completely root out sin or accomplish God's purposes *for* Him. The weight is removed from us, and we are free to trust Him, even amid our own brokenness.

God meets our mustard seed of faith with His vast mercy. He desires us to walk with Him through our pain, to lament before Him in our sorrow. And He doesn't withhold good things when we fall short. So we can't look to the absence of those good things and determine that our faith is weak—or that God is silent.

Reflection Room

Recall: Hebrews 11:1: "Now faith is the assurance of things hoped for, the conviction of things not seen." We're reminded here that God can be trusted regardless of how things appear to us. Would we have need for faith if we, in our own power, could understand everything as it unfolded? The very nature of faith leads us to recognize that what we see may not make sense right now—nor is it a reflection on our worthiness or strength.

Therefore, Remember God's Character

We can't look to circumstances to determine the strength of our faith or God's faithfulness to us. We can't look to the things we see. But if we can't base our faith on the things we see, then what *should* we base it on?

Have you heard of a five-year prayer journal? I hadn't until a few years ago. It's predicated on the notion that you record your prayers over the years on a page dedicated to each day. Then, in subsequent years, you revisit the pages and see the ways God has been faithful to answer and provide. It eliminates short-term memory issues and allows us to see God's goodness on the stage of time. I decided to give it a go.

But three years in, I ran into a problem. I had recorded a lot of small acts of faithfulness. I was thankful. But many of my deepest pleadings seemed to be going unanswered. If anything, the bigger issues were getting worse. Some days, I wanted to replace my few sentences with simply, "Dear God, please see above. And come quickly!"

The psalmist's words seemed to aptly reflect my experience:

> Deep calls to deep
> at the roar of your waterfalls;
> all your breakers and your waves
> have gone over me. (Ps. 42:7)

Life's unrelenting waves just keep crashing over his head. They're loud. They're violent. He feels alone. Later in the psalm (v. 9), he even asks God why he's been forgotten.

His experience felt familiar to me. Where was God in the questions I had poured out on the pages of my journal? And what should I do about it? The psalmist does something unexpected in the midst of his lament: he meditates on the Lord.

> My soul is cast down within me;
>> therefore I remember you
> from the land of Jordan and of Hermon,
>> from Mount Mizar. (Ps. 42:6b)

He hopes not in the *answer* to his prayer but in the *Answerer*—and not because of what God can do for him but because of *who* He is. When we know who the Lord is, our doubts stop where our awe begins. Just as the psalmist chooses to do, we can redirect our energy from our confusion to our praise. And what's more, we can take our questions to God and trust Him with our tender and broken hearts.

God's ways are unsearchable to us, but His character is not. We have a clear picture of who He is and what He's done for us. We have assurance of His consistency. And we know, without a doubt, that His plans will not be thwarted. He doesn't need us to have more faith so that circumstances can change. He desires that we would have more faith so that we can walk in greater peace.

So we're learning to direct our faith to God's character. But practically, what does that look like?

Raw, unbridled, unrestrained faith isn't like a normal "trust fall." It's like throwing your soul headlong off a cliff above a rocky shore and opening yourself up to crushing disappointment. It's vulnerable and terrifying. Real faith is hard because it's foreign. We don't have a perfect human model for what this looks like in practice. The level of trust demanded by real faith is only experienced in communion with the Father. Our human model is broken. People will always disappoint us. They'll always fall short of expectations and let us down in new and often creative ways. Real faith opens the soul to crushing defeat.

But there's good news. God doesn't intend to crush us. In fact, He intends to deliver us from our doubts and disappointment as we find our refuge in Him and not in the things we're clawing after. We enter into real faith knowing that even if His answer is contrary to our deepest longings, it will come with a deeper comfort than anything we've ever experienced. It's a soul-refreshing comfort that our human relationships do not easily demonstrate.

He doesn't need us to have more faith so that circumstances can change. He desires that we would have more faith so that we can walk in greater peace.

The relational model we fall back on is our relationships with people. But people are not the best model for our relationship with the Lord. God will not act in ways that betray His perfect nature. And when we present our requests to Him with a heart that says, "Not my will but Yours be done," He will not disappoint us. Spurgeon writes, "You are not urged to pray in the hour of trouble to experience deeper disappointment."[5] This doesn't mean that the answers to our prayers will be yes or that our faith is weak if they are not. It means that we can take that trust fall of the soul and know that God will catch us.

I want to believe that my friends will be saved. But it's hard to let my mind experience unbridled confidence in God's plan for them. The risk of disappointment is terrifying.

Oh, that the Lord would give us greater faith to trust Him with our hearts, even where His answer might be no. Oh, that the Lord would remind us that He will catch us.

Reflection Room

Wrestle: Does your internal model of trust lead you to base your relationship with God on your experiences with man? Total trust can be terrifying. If you knew that God's plan, timing, and provision would never disappoint you, might you be able to bring to Him any trust you're withholding? Lean into the truth of Jeremiah 29:11 today, and ask Him for a tender heart that runs to Him even in fear. "For I know the plans I have for you, declares the LORD, plans for welfare and not for evil, to give you a future and a hope."

God's Grace Is Sufficient

Know this: We're not falling short in doing our part. There's no cosmic test of faith that keeps the people you love in limbo. Salvation isn't a game, and God isn't manipulating us to seek Him more. He sees you. He sees you seeking, He sees you interceding, and He loves the faith you're cultivating every day.

We can ask for great faith. We can perpetually grow in our faith by God's grace. We can and should pray for and seek such things. But on days when our faith feels small, our God is still big.

The reality is that each of us could have the strongest faith of anyone alive on earth today, and the Lord would still work in His own timing to pursue the hearts of our loved ones. He loves them in spite of them. And He loves them in spite of us. We can praise Him for His mercy, knowing that salvation does not depend on our performance. Just as our works and prayers alone cannot save the people we love, neither can the strength of our faith alone.

The other truth is this: even at our very best, our faith is still shrouded in sin. We do not need to strive for perfection in order for the Lord to hear us. Thank goodness, because otherwise our prayers would fall on deaf ears every time. What we bring to God is total dependence. Our sacrifice on His altar is our striving to control the outcomes. His desire for our faith is that it would rely on Him and not us. That's the whole picture, the whole point. It's not about us at all. It's about God and the sufficiency of His perfect grace.

The question isn't where we end and where God begins—God is, in fact, the beginning, the middle, and the end already. He's working in us and around us, and He is very much a God in the details. When we show up and really get to know Him, we can enjoy all of life as a grand stage on which He presents His finest mercies for us in our weaknesses.

The stage for God's abundant grace is massive because its performance is unlimited.

Prayer Starter

Father, thank You for being the beginning, middle, and end. No insufficiency of mine can thwart Your plans. Please let me see past myself and focus on You and Your character. Thank You for my own salvation, which frees me from my sin. Let me release the burden of guilt that I'm still carrying. Father, would You help me have greater faith? I know Your provision does not depend on me, yet I desire to trust deeply and wholly in You—not to reap some reward, but rather to rest in Your goodness. Thank You that in You there is no disappointment but only deep mercy.

Chapter 10

Will My Loved Ones Be Saved?

Cappuccino. Cheese. Cats. Have you ever thought about how many great words start with the letter *c*?

How about *certainty*? *Clarity. Closure.*

Those three are words of the most delightful comfort and, well, the most perplexing consternation. Certainty. Clarity. Closure. Sweet, yet simple, ideas that seem just out of reach. And so we arrive at the heart of the matter. If we must wait—and if we learn to wait well, with right motives, a heart inclined to the Lord, and a spirit of godly, humble service to and intercession for our people—will any of it really make a difference in the end?

And if not, what's the point?

And is there any way to be sure that God's plans align with our desires, even if we must wait decades for His answer?

Generally speaking, I have two types of friends who don't subscribe to organized religion. Of course, individual viewpoints on the ideas of faith are somewhat different. But for the purposes of discussion, they fall into two broad buckets. Both equally confound me, but for different reasons.

First, there are my agnostic friends like Charlotte and Erin who haven't ultimately ruled out the existence of a higher power or an omnipotent deity but can't get on board with an idea they can't directly see and touch. These friends will engage in philosophical discussions about the universe's origins, the soul and conscience, and ultimate moral truth. They have good questions and aren't opposed to my ideas, even if they find me a bit foolish or misguided.

These friends are perhaps the largest source of my consternation in my journey to trust the Lord. In my seemingly never-ending conversations with Erin about faith and hope and eternal life, not only has she been curious and open-minded, but she's also said she *wants* to believe. She wishes she did believe. By her own account, she's searched for hope and meaning through almost every other avenue, but with no luck.

Perhaps you have friends like this too, who seem to existentially struggle. They wish they could see what you see (even if they simultaneously think you're a bit naive). And in these moments, my confusion is amplified. These lost sons and daughters could be bright lights, publicly professing their newfound hope and freedom, if only they could believe. From what they've shared, it even sounds to me like they'd be excited to believe, like they'd shout it from the rooftops. *So what is God waiting for?*

On the other hand, my atheist friends and family members present a different but much simpler challenge. They aren't curious about religion anymore because to them, the existence of any sort of god is unequivocally fiction. I'm not discouraged as much by their hearts not being inclined toward God as I am by their unwillingness to even open their minds to the possibility of His love for them, let alone His existence. These people don't need "inclinations" toward God; they need total heart overhaul (and perhaps some humility). *So again I ask, what is God waiting for?*

This is the part that will be hard to accept. This is the part where, if it hasn't happened already, the situation will be taken completely out of our hands. It's the part that's a bit exasperating when we've been waiting expectantly for so, so long and it feels impossibly cruel to wait even longer—perhaps even our entire lives. This is the answer I couldn't quite grasp or articulate when I began this journey:

He's waiting until the hearts of the people we love are ready for Him.

> ## Reflection Room
>
> **Wrestle:** Do you trust that God's timing is perfect—that He knows the hearts of your loved ones and is working in their lives? Might there be an area in your waiting journey that isn't fully surrendered? If so, take it daily to God and ask for His help to submit joyfully to His plans and walk in abiding trust.

A Matter of Ripening

Do you bake? I don't find myself baking often, but I have a few favorites I like to whip up from time to time. The other day, I made chocolate chip banana bread. It was terrible. I ate the center right out of it like a bread bowl and threw away the rest of the hard outer shell. My friends told me my bread crisis had something to do with the oven's temperature. But even though the end result was a failure, I did follow the process I was told to follow.

I bought bananas that weren't yet ready for banana bread, and I patiently waited. They were green when I got them. I waited for them to age and soften. It took a bit longer than expected because I keep my home quite cold. (I think I saw snow in here once.) Despite originally planning to bake my banana bread on a Wednesday, I ended up rescheduling my Sunday evening for the project. It was a matter of waiting, of ripening.

In much the same way, the hearts of our friends and family must be softened (sometimes even pulverized) to allow the truth of the gospel admittance into their minds and souls. Closed eyes and hardened hearts will never be able to see the truth. Our loved ones must be ready to taste and see that the Lord is, indeed, good. They must be willing to let in the love He wants to show them. And so, in His infinite wisdom and merciful patience, the Lord is waiting. And so, we are waiting.

But He could cause their hearts to repent tomorrow. The Lord is powerful and mighty. He could cause them to turn to Him, even before allowing them to come to the knowledge of their separation and need. Rather than leading people powerfully but gently to repentance through recognition of their sin nature, He could choose to use His power to skip the refinement process entirely. He could bring about obedience overnight. *So why doesn't He?*

The answer is freedom.

Love without freedom isn't love at all. It's just control. Our Father doesn't intend to control or manipulate us. He desires the closeness of a relationship governed by genuine interest, love, and free will.

Have you ever raised anything up with love and patience? Kids, pets, plants? I don't have children yet, but I do have two cats. Sometimes they like to live their own lives, separate from mine—ridiculous, I know. When I'm relaxing alone in the living room, I'll get lonely and go in search of them. I want attention and affection, and that is one of their main jobs. I often find them in the bathroom sink or playing under the bed, where all their toys inevitably end up. Or rubbing up against all the professional clothes in my closet, as part of what is surely a plot to keep the lint roller business booming.

Our Father doesn't intend to control or manipulate us. He desires the closeness of a relationship governed by genuine interest, love, and free will.

I'm bigger and stronger than my cats, so once I find them, I pick them up and whisk them away to a place of my choosing. They are never pleased. I cuddle them while they squirm and eventually win the fight for escape, the battle for freedom.

I did not create my cats. They were not made in my image. I saw them up for adoption at a local rescue organization and basically bought them on the internet! And yet, I delight in their affection and want to spend time with them. And what's more, I want them to *want to* spend time with me. How much more does our Father in heaven, who ordained our very existence, forming us in His image in order to live in relationship with Him, desire that we freely choose to love Him? We are far more valuable than cats.

There is no fear in love, but perfect love drives out fear (1 John 4:18). In a relationship where one party governs by means of total control, we will always experience fear and apprehension.

We have all been given individual freedom to pursue *ultimate* freedom. Submission to the Lord in the context of His fatherly love is freedom and protection in its purest form.

Galatians 5:1 reminds us, "For freedom Christ has set us free; stand firm therefore, and do not submit again to a yoke of slavery." He didn't intend for us to live with unholy fear or to be forced into submission. In fact, God sent His Son, Jesus Christ, to give the ultimate sacrifice—His life—by dying on a cross. He did this to bear the weight of sin so that we wouldn't have to. He did this so that we would be free. He did this because of how deeply He loves us. And He didn't ask for anything in return. It was a gift freely given.

We can trust a Father who loves us so purely and deeply that He sent His Son to die for us. We can trust the boundary lines He's encouraged us to live within. We can trust that He does not intend to harm us but to protect us and to greatly supply us with His providence.

Ironically, the road of rebellion is far more encumbered than the road of obedience. It is existential crisis at its finest. This is because the Lord, in perfect love for us, desires only our eternal good. There is no fear and no yoke of slavery in submission to a God whose love is perfect, free, and redemptive.

An unjust god wouldn't think twice about demanding total submission, exerting dominance over our hearts and actions, and turning us to him in worship. An unjust god would force us to our knees before him. But if love is freedom, our God demonstrates perfect love by giving us free will.

There was one consistent conclusion in my conversations with Charlotte about God. We'd get to the end of all our postulating and pontificating, and she would boldly declare that if there was a god up there, then after examining the cruelty in the world, the pain in her own life, and the observed misery and suffering experienced by humanity, this was no god she would want to worship. To her, that would be an unjust god, indeed.

The irony to me is that an unjust god, if he did exist, wouldn't even let her have such an opinion—or would smite her if she did. An unjust god would demand total obedience and devotion. He wouldn't deliver us from the sins of humanity but use them against us. An evil, unjust god would never impart freedom, and he would certainly not be characterized by love. Our perspective of the destruction sin causes in the world actually points us back to God's goodness rather than away from it. Without His mercy, we would be wholly consumed.

Even so, some of our friends haven't yet realized the extent of God's love for them. It is my earnest prayer that everyone for whom we are praying will be saved and reconciled to God through Christ. I do know, though, that it is possible that one or more of them will take another path. Some hearts will not turn toward the Lord.

It is, ironically, a right they have been given by God Himself. It is perhaps the height of pride. There is nothing we will be able to do for those who ultimately choose this path of destruction.

To the best of our ability, though, we should not be consumed with fear and worry that this will be the fate of our loved ones. Instead, we can trust that the Lord loves them deeply and knows the deepest inclinations of their hearts.

He is perfectly wise and discerning; He has complete knowledge and righteous judgment. He won't get it wrong. It is my wholehearted belief that the Lord will pursue His lost sheep to the very ends of the earth. And what's more, God will be very patient with them.

Luke 15:10 tells us, "Just so, I tell you, there is joy before the angels of God over one sinner who repents." Even one life saved is cause for elation and celebration in the kingdom of heaven. God is planning many joyous celebrations.

Reflection Room

Reframe: Instead of allowing this season of waiting to be clouded with frustration or confusion, accept the Lord's invitation to walk in the very freedom that He is offering your loved ones. But instead of using that freedom to go your own way or grasp at perceived control over the situation, choose to use it to trust Him more fully and to rest more peacefully, recognizing that He is good. What is He calling you to release to Him today as you wait?

Invited to Wait

I know you deeply desire the answer to this chapter's question. But in your moments of pain, resentment, hopelessness, or doubt, have you ever asked yourself, *What would happen if I didn't feel this way?*

What if I weren't focusing so much on the salvation of others? Would I carry on in a state of resigned indifference, halfheartedly whispering a brief prayer for the lost on rare days when the thought happened to cross my mind? To be honest, consistent prayer for lost people wasn't always at the top of my to-do list before the pandemic.

The Lord took away my plans, much of my community, and almost all my routines. He showed me what I'd been missing before—this invitation I'd ignored and buried under other "priorities." Maybe that's how this pain came upon you as well ... or maybe you've been carrying it for much longer.

I realize now that what I once considered a painful burden was actually God inviting me into a season of deep intimacy with Him. The weakness I hated so much was actually God inviting me to experience His power. What I once considered confusing I now realize was the lifting of a veil of delightful ignorance, in which I spent a lot less time with God and a lot more time prioritizing my to-do list. His light shone into the dark, distracted places of my heart and left me with greater care for my friends and family and greater awareness of the depth of His love for all His image bearers.

We can count it as a great privilege that the Lord has placed this burden on our hearts. Pain on this side of heaven, in many ways, is one of God's greatest mercies. This burden we feel for the people we love isn't a hindrance; it's an invitation. God invites us into this conversation with Him and assures us that He's here to listen. He loves our deep care for these lost people because He shares it, and He doesn't intend for us to shoulder it alone. Our pain, when submitted wisely to Him, conforms us to Christ.

He loves our deep care for these lost people because He shares it, and He doesn't intend for us to shoulder it alone.

I thought I could've gone without the burden. That I could've gone on living better without such deep concern. But as it turns out, it wouldn't have been the kind of life that honored my friends and family quite as well before God.

We certainly don't want to exist in a perpetual state of despair, but God doesn't want us to become apathetic either. We can learn to give our questions and confusion to the Lord. We can pray *specifically*, *earnestly*, and *consistently* for our lost friends and family members by name and thank God for His invitation to join Him on the journey.

Maybe your internal struggle isn't always as intense as mine. Maybe you haven't been angry at God like I was. Maybe you haven't harbored resentment like I did for something I have no control over. I couldn't shake my frustration over the unknown. But I learned that we can delight in the intimacy that the Lord is inviting us into without having to fully understand or have any control over the outcome.

We can trust Him with our cares and confusion, our frustration and our doubt. Day after day after day.

Reflection Room

Request: Lord, thank You for affliction that refines me and conforms me to Christ's likeness. Would You please give me the peace to walk in the freedom to which You have called me? I trust You. I want to believe. Remind me that my concern for my loved ones is an invitation to receive Your care. Thank You for allowing me the grand privilege of sharing Your love for lost people.

Peace in His Presence

Evil is devastating. But it's not surprising. I always come back to Genesis 6:5, which tells us, "The LORD saw that the wickedness of man was great in the earth, and that every intention of the thoughts of his heart was only evil continually."

Wicked hearts must be reconciled with the Father, who freely gave His gift of salvation. The good news is that in waiting for hearts to become ready, the Lord is working. He has not left anyone alone or abandoned them. He isn't sitting idly by. Even as you read this book, know that the Lord has sent *you* to your friends and family on mission for Him. Our relationships are no mistake, and God is not surprised by the paths our lives take or the people we meet on the way.

In waiting for the salvation of my fearfully and wonderfully made friends, I have come to the end of me. I have reached the limits of my ability to carry the burdens and to endure their separation. But at the end of me, at the end of my abilities, at the very end of my road, is my Father, who is able. If you are at the end, know that He is with you. At the end of ourselves, there is freedom. There is the beginning of a vast, unlimited God.

If we're not sure that God loves our friends and family, and if we just aren't sure how to fully trust Him with all of it, we would be wise to reflect on God's consistent faithfulness to us.

Early in my writing journey I realized I had a serious problem. Much of what I'd written seemed good and true, but there was a huge obstacle standing in the way of my continuing. For a long time, I'd been running from a prohibitive truth hiding inside the dark places in my mind: I didn't *really* trust God with the lives of the lost people I loved.

I wanted to. I had worked my way through some of my questions. Everything I'd written sounded like good ideas for anyone who *could* trust Him. And I was trying my best. I had all the head knowledge of God's love, and I believed in the inerrant words of Scripture. I knew a lot of things to be true … but living out that belief through trust in a heavenly Father requires more than just head knowledge. I realized that it would be hard to continue writing unless something changed. But I didn't know how to cultivate trust on my own.

Unbeknownst to me, in the year preceding my writing, the Lord had been showing up in my life in order to communicate not only His affection for me but also His intentional, faithful pursuit of me. I didn't realize what was happening while I was living through it. Trusted friends and advisers spoke into the circumstances they observed in my life, and I realized the extent to which the Lord had been pursuing me daily with exceeding gentleness and tenderness. In my case, He demonstrated His care through other people's love when I needed it most. But at first, I'd just attributed His care entirely to them instead!

There have been several occasions in the past when I have experienced the Lord's provision and love but never so much as over the course of that year. I wept at the revelation that I had attributed so much of the goodness I had experienced to sources other than God. Even when those circumstances had passed, God wanted to meet me where I was, every day, without exception and without condemnation. His love and pursuit of me were overwhelming, and Psalm 139 came to mind:

> How precious to me are your thoughts, O God!
> How vast is the sum of them! (v. 17)

If we're not sure that God loves our friends and family, and if we just aren't sure how to fully trust Him with all of it, we would be wise to reflect on God's consistent faithfulness to us. In the revelation of God's gentle, continual, and relational pursuit of me, I experienced security in my relationship with Him and freedom in knowing He's pursuing the lost people I love as well. This is a God who is intentional and faithful.

For lasting freedom from despair over lost hearts, look at how the Lord has shown up in your own life time and time again. And if you can't see that, ask that He would make you aware of His presence there. Ask Him to be exceedingly gentle with you. Rest in the truth of Matthew 11:28–30, where Christ promises, "Come to me, all who labor and are heavy laden, and I will give you rest. Take my yoke upon you, and learn from me, for I am gentle and lowly in heart, and you will find rest for your souls. For my yoke is easy, and my burden is light."

When we realize the extent of the Lord's affection for us as our Father, it's not hard to see how much He loves everyone else too. It's okay if it's hard to feel His affection in some moments. Let's take the time we need to explore His character, learn His promises, and understand His intentions. Let's commit to spending consistent time with Him. It's hard to cultivate trust in a moment. Trust is built over time, through relationship. Trust is built when we see promises lived out. Time spent with God cultivates trust in His nature and character. We experience peace in His presence. And thus we come to hope in who He is. Hope is built on a foundation of trust and buttressed by love, patience, and grand mercy.

Reflection Room

Recall: Ephesians 3:18–19, in which Paul expresses to the Ephesians his desire that they "may have power, together with all the Lord's holy people, to grasp how wide and long and high and deep is the love of Christ, and to know this love that surpasses knowledge—that you may be filled to the measure of all the fullness of God" (NIV).

The same holds true for you. As you read the Bible, consider highlighting verses that speak of God's love, affection, and care for you. In moments of doubt or uncertainty, revisit these passages and remember that even when head knowledge is insufficient, His love far exceeds reason.

We Know All That We Need to Know

And so, I end with a few final thoughts: God sees the hearts of all those we love dearly. He sees whether there is still a stubbornness and a self-sufficiency that would reject Him. He doesn't merely know when the hearts of our loved ones *might* be ready for Him. Rather, He is *making* them ready in His time. But He is gentle and tender toward them. Heart change takes time. He is moving and working and preparing minds to receive Him in ways that reveal and express the ultimate love that is given to all who turn to Him. We don't need to understand everything that God is doing when we understand who He is.

I'd posit that in requesting answers about eternity, we are asking the wrong questions. Instead of asking whether the eternal destiny of our loved ones rests on our shoulders, here are some questions we might ask instead:

- Do we believe that the Lord loves us?
- Do we believe that He loves our loved ones?

- Do we really believe that the Lord is in control of all things?
- Do we trust in His timing and His plan?
- Do we need answers to all our questions in order to keep believing, to keep trusting?
- Do we believe that the Lord is good?

I'll be honest with you. In the end, the answer to the question of whether God will save our loved ones is *I don't know.* I don't know what God will do. But what I do know is that that isn't the most important question. And even if we had all the answers, more information would not ultimately bring us peace. Our hope is not found in answers. Our hope is found in the goodness of God and His unlimited love for us and for all people.

While some things are not ours to know, we can take heart in the truth that we know all that we need to know.

Prayer Starter

Merciful, mighty, sovereign Lord, thank You that You are God and I am not. Thank You that You intimately know the hearts of my lost friends and family members. Thank You that You love them more than I can even possibly imagine. Please, I beg, free me from fear and worry over their eternities, and draw me into Your deep care when my heart is troubled. Remind me who You are and that You hold the people I love in Your very hands. Refine me in my pain, and remind me also of Your deep love for *me*. Please grow our relationship and strengthen my trust in You. Father, I humbly ask for Your deep and abiding peace as I wait in hope for the people I love to know and worship You alongside me.

Conclusion

Every day for the past forty-nine months, I've prayed for my friend Charlotte.

When I first started writing the words that eventually became this book, that sentence read *eight*. Eight months. As of this writing, it's forty-nine, and I am still waiting for Charlotte's freedom. And unless you've experienced a long-awaited miracle during the time you've been reading this book, you're still waiting also. Take heart, dear friend. You are not alone.

I started writing about this pain on August 17, 2020. True to my accountant's nature, I kept a spreadsheet to track my progress. To be honest, I'm not sure why I did that—I had no idea it would become a book, much less a published one. My counselor even told me I referred to my writing for several months as "the document." According to the spreadsheet, I wrote 3.02 percent of the document that first day of writing. By early November, I'd written more than 70 percent of my initial manuscript draft.

But on November 12, 2020, I walked away from it. The doubt was overwhelming. I couldn't keep track of the increasing word count, and I just couldn't see the point of continuing to write. It wouldn't change anything.

Over a year passed before I sat down to write again on a random work night in January 2022. The previous Sunday, my pastor had preached a message on thorns in the flesh. Thorns can take many shapes, he'd said: physical ailment, social impairment, spiritual persecution, or really any other ongoing pain or struggle that feels limiting or debilitating.

For me, I'd say the depth of the pain I experience on account of my lost friends is my thorn. If that sounds like an overly righteous thing to say, rest assured that I don't always bear my thorn well. It's a nearly constant battle for hope, trust, and peace. It requires me to open my hands every morning at the same time I open my eyes.

But, as with all the thorns, it keeps me humble. And at the end of every day, it's that thorn that drives me to my knees before the Lord. The Lord uses thorns for His glory and to draw us to His strength, encouraging us to rely on Him alone.

What if things don't turn out the way I would write the story? What if this thorn remains for the rest of my life?

The reality is this: We don't get to know how the story ends. But we do get to control where we direct our energy along the way. We *can* use our thorns to glorify God. While the ending may be outside our control, what we have to offer to the Lord is our heart.

I've learned not to throw away my tenderness before the Lord on account of what He's doing in the lives and hearts and minds of other people. I am accountable only for mine, and you are accountable only for yours.

We could succumb to bitterness toward God for things we don't understand—in fact, I've tried that. The only result I reaped was misery. So every day I do my best to choose tenderness before God. This tenderness doesn't come by accident. It comes from steadfast pursuit. It comes, quite literally, from crying out to God and begging Him for that tenderness. I open my hands before my Father in dust and ashes.

Every day, I will let my thorn drive me humbly to my knees before Him, unless He should choose to remove it. I have nothing to offer but a tender and obedient heart that says, "Here I am." And His grace is sufficient for me.

In the scheme of life, my pain is young. My most earnest, pleading prayers for the lost people I love have consumed only the last few years. There are many believers who've carried this thorn for decades. I've imagined what that might be like, since, as far as I can tell, that's where I'm headed. This brought to mind Paul's words: "Let us not become weary in doing good, for at the proper time we will reap a harvest if we do not give up" (Gal. 6:9 NIV).

Bearing in mind the road ahead, I'm all the more encouraged to accept the grace God has for me each day as I open my hands to His sovereignty and let my thorns drive me to my knees before Him.

When we serve our friends faithfully out of the overflow of God's great love, when we approach Him with open hands, submitting their lives to Him, when we seek God first and take to Him our desires for the salvation of the lost, when we worship Him and place no idols— even salvation—above Him, we will surely experience the abundance of the harvest. *The harvest we reap is peace.*

We may experience harvests of many kinds. We don't know what the future harvest entails in all its bounty. But we do know where we're headed. And we know who's there waiting to welcome us home.

In a life full of brokenness and disappointment, unmet expectations and sorrow, the best gifts from God aren't the tangible things

we want in the moments in which we want them—not even the godli-
est things. The best things produced in the harvest are the steadfast
endurance and abiding peace that come *despite* all the things that are
not the way they should be in this life.

> The reality is this: We don't
> get to know how the story
> ends. But we do get to control
> where we direct our energy
> along the way. We _can_ use
> our thorns to glorify God.

As I was writing this book, I wasn't sure if there would be a
market for the topic. Before a few years ago, I was living in a state of
busy indifference to the eternities of people around me. I loved my
friends and family, and I hoped they would choose to follow Christ.
But next to those thoughts were many other thoughts ... like my
Friday night dinner plans, my presentation coming up at work, and
the errands that were on my agenda each day. I prayed for my lost
friends but nowhere near as earnestly, as often, or as consistently as
I do now.

I assumed that a few others might be a lot like me, living with this
struggle just a bit off the radar, placing it in a pile of other less-than-
ideal things about the world we're living in. Life is busy and distracting.
So I wasn't sure if there were very many.

Amid the pandemic, my church continued our monthly congregational meetings using a video meeting platform. One evening in late 2020, about eighty-five people tuned in for prayer, congregational updates, and fellowship. We spent the first half of the meeting in corporate prayer.

We prayed deeply and earnestly for a few topics as a church. Afterward, my pastor opened the floor, asking us to use the chat feature to share with our congregation specific things for which we needed prayer. Our intent was to pray as a body for the difficult things that we were all walking through. I flipped over to the chat, expecting to see prayer requests for peace in unemployment or sickness or depression—or really any of the many real, painful, and difficult circumstances we were all experiencing.

Much to my surprise, I watched as request after request poured into the chat. None of them were for any of the things I had expected to see. Each request was for the salvation of beloved friends and family who were apart from God. Every painful plea that filled my screen asked our church body if we could please pray for people to be saved.

My heart broke for all the others who were waiting. But I also rejoiced that amid global turmoil, personal pain, and a season of unexpected and uncomfortable life change, the other believers on the call that night felt that the saving of lives for the glory of God was of the utmost importance. I felt assured, then, that others were feeling the same way as I did and that, truly, none of us were alone in our seasons of waiting.

We lifted to the Lord the names of our friends and family members that day. All eighty-five of us in consecrated prayer for specific lost people whom we dearly love. I submitted Charlotte's name too, of course, and the joy that filled my heart upon hearing her name spoken in prayer can hardly be expressed.

I considered the things outside of the meeting that I had done that week, and it was apparent that *there was no greater commission than this.* As we bowed our heads in humble submission before the Lord, praying earnestly that our people might be saved and become disciples, taking His Word to the nations, I realized that this was our greatest calling. And just as we're told at the end of Matthew 28:16–20 in the Great Commission itself, the Lord was *with* us. He heard each and every name.

Truly, in comparison to knowing God, I count everything as loss. We want that same joy for our sweet friends and family. We long for that deeply. We weep for them at the feet of God.

Keep praying, keep interceding, and keep weeping with total trust in Him. If you walk away from this book with only one thing, let it be encouragement that you and your people are at the center of the very will of God and that He is with you. He will deal very gently with you. He hears you.

In seeking first God and His will for their lives, and especially in trusting Him, you edify your friends, yourself, and the kingdom.

Child of God and fellow believer, how deeply the King of the universe loves your friends and family. In His good design, He ordained from the beginning of time their very existence. He loves the people we love more than you and I love them combined, more than our combined imaginations can possibly fathom. He knows what they need and when they need it. Mercifully, their salvation is not for us to decide or obtain. Be released from their struggle.

Be free to love the Lord with all your heart and all your soul and all your mind. And then be free to love the people around you without the burden of their eternities on your shoulders. Be free and know that the God of the universe is in control, and He is writing a very redemptive story. He desires deeply that you would have peace in your waiting, as you walk the road of loving people who don't love God.

A Prayer for the Lost People We Love

Here you'll find an example prayer of intercession for your friends and family. I hope this will be a tool you can use as you take the names of your loved ones to the Lord. Remember, He hears each and every name, so I encourage you to pray for each person who is on your heart by replacing the name Charlotte with the names of those you love.

Father, thank You for ____*Charlotte*____ .

Thank You that her very life is the work of Your hand. That she is Your creation, made in Your image. Thank You that You formed her in her mother's womb and that You have marked and counted the minutes of her life. Thank You for the great, unmatched privilege of bringing her name before You.

Lord, please pursue her powerfully. Please cause her to begin to wonder, to question, to get curious. Please bring her to the end of her own strength. Let her notice Your mysteries in the world around her and begin to grapple with your lordship. Place compelling resources and testimonies in her path, and turn her eyes toward You. Orchestrate encounters that point her to You and Your kingdom. Let Your servants show up in her life and love her well on Your account. Please reveal Yourself to her. Let her know You.

Please soften her heart and open her eyes. Please cause her to bring before You her sin and her shame and her brokenness. Let her fall on her knees before You in repentance. Let her worship You as Lord.

Please save ___Charlotte___. And then, please make fruitful the work of her hands. Let her life count for the saving of many. Please produce in her wisdom and holiness and godliness that glorifies You and spreads Your gospel to the nations. Draw her into unmatched intimacy with You and sanctify her by Your Spirit. Father, please let her experience the vastness of Your mercy.

Please rescue Your daughter, who is precious to You.

Thank You that You are working. That You love her dearly.

___Charlotte___, whom You formed; ___Charlotte___, whom we love.

Thank You, merciful, sovereign Father, that Your Son, Jesus, died for ___Charlotte___.

May she know the Truth, and may her name be written in the Book of Life.

Please let me see Your goodness in the land of the living. Lord, I wait with deep and abiding hope for her salvation. I cry out to You desperately to save my friend. Please comfort me, encourage me, and uplift me as I wait. But, Lord, I trust You with the trajectory of her life.

I submit and release my will to You, Most High God. Your will be done.

In the mighty, matchless name of Jesus, amen.

Acknowledgments

This book was first and foremost written through the power of the Spirit. I was not previously a writer, nor am I employed in any sort of creative arts. My education and work history are, bewilderingly, in the field of accounting. And what's more, I am not particularly experienced, even in that field. I truly believe that the Lord called me to the writing of this book so that those who know me would be encouraged in faith that all things are possible with God. They can certainly attest that this was not written in my own strength. Of course, I take all responsibility for any errors in translating ideas.

Each time I sat down to write, the Lord would direct me to a passage for the evening, and upon scrolling to the appropriate chapter, the words would come. I was given a little for each day that I wrote. The chapters came about one small portion at a time but truly with the greatest of ease. *The call to write was not a call for me to speak but rather a call to listen.*

I recall one evening early in the writing process when I had reached 24.88 percent of my total word-count goal. I was eager to reach the 25 percent mark and experience the glee of having drafted one-fourth of an actual book. But the Lord made it clear to me that I had finished all He had for me that day, and I was free to carry on with my evening.

Two days later, He laid upon my heart another passage, which pushed me over the 27 percent threshold. Things didn't always go according to my timeline. But His was far better.

I am most thankful to my merciful Father for giving me this project on which to focus my time and attention. It was not only enjoyable and engaging but restorative and fulfilling amid a deeply painful season. In the process, there was healing.

God's answers to my prayers about my pain and confusion weren't the immediate salvation of my lost friends but instead the lessons He taught me as I wrote this book, which have enabled me to receive sustaining peace and, God willing, to share it with others who are also waiting. If none should ever read it but me, still it was a great blessing, which I did not earn but which God graciously gave to me out of His deep love. My relationship with the Lord has been strengthened from the time we spent together working on this project. Truly, I have seen the depth of His faithfulness.

All remaining thanks goes out to the following children of God, without whom this book would not exist:

To David C Cook and all the good stewards of God's varied grace who've been called to their publishing ministry—thank you for taking a chance on me. This journey held so much joy. To Susan McPherson and Stephanie Bennett for so kindly guiding me through the process and encouraging me every step of the way. I am so incredibly lucky to have worked with you. Thank you for your belief in this message. I'm grateful for your faithful work in giving writers like me a place from which to share the words on our hearts that we might shine Christ's light in dark places. You are truly a city set on a hill.

To my editor, Julie Cantrell, for your patience, partnership, and great care for my message. I am in awe of your exceptional editorial skill and deeply appreciative of your mentorship. Your guidance throughout this process has been invaluable, and I will carry the things you've taught me into all my future work. Thank you for the effort you poured into this book and for being a guiding light in my journey as a writer.

To Eric Saunders, Joe Carter, David Platt, Mike Kelsey, and all the faithful pastors at my church who shepherd our congregation well for the glory of God and the spread of the gospel in the world. Your leadership and wisdom are among God's greatest blessings in my life. I am extremely lucky to be here in this time and this place, experiencing the fruit of your gifts and your labor. It is a vast and undeserved privilege to sit beneath your teaching each week.

I'd like to extend special thanks to Pastor Joe for your time spent reviewing my manuscript and providing your thoughtful feedback, even within the confines of my tight deadline. I so deeply appreciate your wisdom and insight.

To Sarah Bruce, for your wise and biblical counsel. I am thankful for your servant's heart. You listened to me at length and continually and graciously pointed me back to the nature and character of God. Your deep empathy and nonjudgmental spirit not only paved the way for much growth and maturation but, more importantly, taught me, above all else, to seek refuge in God and to remember, always, that He is good.

To Dr. Lee Warren, for responding to an email from a stranger asking for writing advice. Your genuine, kind encouragement was a great act of service that propelled me into finally sitting down to write the very first words.

To the Christian music artists whose lyrics and works encourage me, lift me up, and inspire me to rejoice in praise. Thank you for your service to the kingdom.

To my mom, who probably found it quite random and surprising that her daughter wrote a book (although probably not as surprising as it was to me). Thank you for your unconditional love and unending support. You reflect God's grace. There is no greater gift on this side of heaven that God could've given me than you (apart from Christ Himself, certainly). You are a bright and shining light that has never once flickered. I love you with as strong a love as can possibly be felt by a human heart. Who am I that He is mindful of me?

To my dad, for all the ways you've supported me, even when I unexpectedly quit my job to work on a book, get another degree, and redirect my career focus. It wouldn't have been possible without you. I love you, and I'm thankful beyond what I can express in words. Wisdom you shared years ago still resonates with me. When I voiced my concern that an upcoming project might be quite challenging, you replied, "Anything that's worth it usually is." I'm grateful for your example, which spurs me on in discipline and perseverance.

To Katherine, for your delightful, miraculous gift of friendship— a direct answer to years of prayer. Thank you for your grace-filled, patient listening as I processed deep and intense pain. You are truly a sister for adversity. Your heart for others and for me points me back to Jesus, and I dearly love you. You are one of life's greatest harbingers of hope.

To Amy, my dear friend of nearly twenty years, who was even more excited than I was that I wrote a book. Your patient, loyal, and enduring friendship is one of the great joys of my life. It is a privilege to know you.

And finally, to Charlotte, for your loyal and steadfast friendship. The deepest desire of my heart is to know and glorify God. The second deepest desire is that you would know Him too. This book is for you.

Notes

Chapter 1: This Situation Feels Unfair

1. Matthew 10:14.

Chapter 5: This Pain Feels Too Deep

1. Eric Saunders, "Our Mission Statement, Part 3—Arlington," January 19, 2020, in *McLean Bible Church*, podcast, MP3 audio, 32:53, https://podcasts.apple.com /us/podcast/mclean-bible-church-audio-podcast/id990724465?i=1000463103121.

2. Sarah McLachlan, "Angel," on *Surfacing*, Nettwerk, 1997.

3. C. H. Spurgeon, *Beside Still Waters*, ed. Roy H. Clarke (Nashville, TN: Thomas Nelson, 1999), 31.

Chapter 7: Does God Hear My Prayers?

1. C. H. Spurgeon, *Beside Still Waters*, ed. Roy H. Clarke (Nashville, TN: Thomas Nelson, 1999), 265.

2. Eric Saunders, "Our Mission Statement, Part 3—Arlington," January 19, 2020, in *McLean Bible Church*, podcast, MP3 audio, 26:10, https://podcasts.apple.com /us/podcast/mclean-bible-church-audio-podcast/id990724465?i=1000463103121.

3. Spurgeon, *Beside Still Waters*, 100.

Chapter 8: How Do I Wait Victoriously?

1. C. H. Spurgeon, *Beside Still Waters*, ed. Roy H. Clarke (Nashville, TN: Thomas Nelson, 1999), 120.

2. "It Is Well with My Soul—Spafford Hymn," Spafford Hymn, accessed September 15, 2023, www.spaffordhymn.com.

3. C. S. Lewis, *Mere Christianity* (San Francisco: HarperOne, 1952), 227.

Chapter 9: What Role Does My Faith Play?

1. Mark Vroegop, *Dark Clouds, Deep Mercy: Discovering the Grace of Lament* (Wheaton, IL: Crossway, 2019), 18.

2. Vroegop, *Dark Clouds, Deep Mercy*, 28.

3. Vroegop, *Dark Clouds, Deep Mercy*, 28.

4. Vroegop, *Dark Clouds, Deep Mercy*, 95–96.

5. C. H. Spurgeon, *Beside Still Waters*, ed. Roy H. Clarke (Nashville, TN: Thomas Nelson, 1999), 85.